PERSONAL FINANCE

SIX SIMPLE STEPS TO TAKE FULL CONTROL OF YOUR FINANCES, GAIN FINANCIAL FREEDOM, AND RETIRE EARLY

OA INC

CONTENTS

GIFT

Just For You!

A FREE GIFT TO OUR READERS
Tips for managing your personal finance that you can
download and begin to implement right away! Visit this link:

http://oainc.activehosted.com/f/1

INTRODUCTION

A fresh graduate with a huge education loan started his first job with a decent salary and aimed to clear off his debt as soon as possible. But he was stuck in the same job for a long period as the loan kept piling on month after month. Does this sound familiar? How many of you have bought things on impulse but when you come home, you realise that you did not need them? Do you find yourself living paycheck to paycheck? Or when surprises turn up, like a medical emergency or vehicle problems, you end up asking for a loan. Most of us have fallen into the trap of improper financial planning and have ended up paying a huge price for it. But do not stress as it is never too late to start looking after your personal finances.

In all these scenarios, money is the common factor. Most importantly, you need an adequate amount of money at the right time to fulfill all your dreams and goals. This is where financial planning comes into the picture. As companies have long-term and short-term plans to look after their expenditures, in personal life too you require planning to lead a stress-free life.

THE IMPORTANCE OF PLANNING YOUR PERSONAL FINANCES

Wealth creation: The price of everyday items is increasing and to maintain your current lifestyle, you need to create a sizable corpus of funds. In future, you may want to buy a house or get married; this will require money, which will be in addition to your daily requirements. This itself highlights the importance of financial planning. You can earn the amount by investing your money in the right avenues ("Importance Of Financial Planning," n.d.).

Increase your savings: Financial planning takes into account your income from all sources and from your expenditures. This provides necessary insights into your unnecessary expenses and will guide you to curtail them. This step will automatically increase your savings in the long run.

Be better prepared for emergencies: While planning your budget, creating a fund for emergencies is a vital part of this process. The current pandemic has taught us that emergencies can strike anyone at any point. It is important to keep a minimum of six months of your salary as an emergency fund. This fund can help you sail your ship during a medical emergency or a job loss. This will avoid you further stress to look out for avenues to fund your emergency.

Personal finance planning gives you the necessary peace of mind. When you have planned for your future, and set aside funds for emergencies, and with adequate funds in your hand to help you with your daily expenses, you can live your life without any worry. Financial planning helps you reach that stage. Do not fret if you have not reached that stage; having the intent is the first step towards achieving financial independence and living a stress-free life.

Retirement planning: Whether you have just started your job or you may be mid-career, it is important to start planning for your retirement. You need to start preparing your safety net now to let you live a happy and comfortable retired life. While planning for your retirement, the most important cost will be your medical expenses. With life span increasing post-retirement, you will require a larger amount of money compared to your ancestors. Also, if you start early, you can build a large corpus of money over 25 to 30 years with the power of compounding.

Beat inflation: You know how our grandparents reminisce that 20 years ago, things were cheaper? The price for a movie ticket that you paid five years ago must have doubled by now. This phenomenon of increase in price over the years is called inflation. Wondering why you should worry about inflation? Suppose you have $1,000 in your savings account and the rate of interest on your savings account is 5%. That means next year you will have $1,050 in your account. Now if the inflation rate is 10%, you would need $1100 in your account to have the same buying capacity.

So, this means if your savings do not increase at the same rate as the inflation, you will end up losing money.

Apart from the above-mentioned reasons, financial planning also helps manage your portfolio better. You can see which savings scheme is giving you better returns, what is the risk factor in each savings scheme, and then tweak your plan as required.

You may have several different goals to achieve, but if you have not planned your finances properly, you will not be able to achieve any of them. Hence, sound personal finance planning is important. In the next few chapters, we will understand the basics of financial planning, and how proper debt management can help you to reduce the interest you end up paying to your creditors. We will also learn the art of investing, and how the right investments can help in securing your future.

Over the years, I have worked with many customers who were struggling with huge loans and credit card bills. I understood the issues and worked on a plan that eventually got them on the right track. Most importantly, I have been in debt and was successful in navigating myself and coming out debt-free. This book is my attempt to share knowledge that I have gained over the years and support you in your path to financial freedom.

BUDGETING

The process of balancing our income with our expenses is called budgeting. It is a way to plan to manage our expenses and your money. It allows us to plan for future spendings and gives us an idea to prioritize our expenditure, save money for future needs, and keep us out of debt. Many of us think budgeting is about spending less, whereas its actual purpose is to spend less than we earn.

To keep our finances on track, we must learn how to spend less than we earn. Thus, we must plan and map our spendings. By doing this, we can forecast our spendings and savings. One must always have a realistic expense tracker and be honest about their income and expenses, as this may help in long-term financial planning and keep us out of debt. Financial planning allows us to fulfill our short- and long-term goals like buying a vehicle, going on a vacation or buying a house, and planning our retirement. One must always plan and know their expenses. Not paying attention to the budget may lead to unpaid bills, maxed-out credit cards, debt, and most importantly, mental stress.

Good financial planning has lots of perks: good vacations, dinner parties with friends and family, paying off loans, emergency funds for unexpected expenses like medical bills, back up money in case you lose your job. All these can happen if there is good budgeting and all one needs to do is to track their weekly/monthly expenses, note them down, and track and control any unusual expenditure.

Budgeting also makes us aware of bad spending habits. It will help to recognise a pattern if you are spending on items that you do not need. For example, it will make you wonder if you really need that tenth pair of shoes or to order food five nights in a row? Budgeting will force you to rethink your spending habits and shift your focus back to your financial goals.

How many of you have spent sleepless nights wondering how to clear the long-due credit card bill or to source funds for the sudden emergency? People lose their mental peace and sleep over financial stress. Do not allow money to control you; instead, learn how to control your money. Budgeting helps in getting back that control and also gets your sleep back.

BUDGETING TIPS

Budgeting may sound complicated but on the contrary, it isn't if we know where our money is going. It is about knowing your needs and your expenses. It does not matter how much one earns; one must know how to allocate their funds in the best possible way. Even if our finances are in good shape and order, good budgeting may surprise us by letting us discover some hidden issues with the finances and help us spend and save more wisely. Before we start budgeting, we must think about the future goals. What do we wish to accomplish in the coming few years with the money? It may be a plan to start your own business, to get married, to start a family, pay off loans, or move to a new city/country. At the same time, it is important for us to have short-term plans too.

The first step towards budgeting is to have the intentions. Having concrete and clear intentions will help you plan your budget in the best way, and you are more likely to stick to the plan. At first, it may seem difficult and confusing. Always remember to start with the basics. You should then note down your fixed and variable expenses like house rent/loan, groceries, travel expenses, and subscriptions. One can do it manually or use software and apps like Mint, Personal Capital, and others to enter the data (Dore, n.d.). The plus point with these apps is that it analyses your data and presents it under different sections. This analysis will help to understand your spending habits better and can also act as a reminder to be on the right track (Vohwinkle, 2009).

Once the budget has been created, then comes the tricky part of tracking it. This tracking plays a key role in your future financial plans.

We need to track the budget on a monthly basis for at least three to six months. This tracking will help you identify weaknesses in your budget, and then appropriate action can be taken to cut or add the amount in any particular segment.

One should avoid making big changes or cuts in the budget in the initial months, as the changes need to be gradual. The budget can be further adjusted in the future. Remember the rule that it is okay to spend more in a certain segment, but make sure to adjust it within the budget rather than putting in more from your pocket.

To progress in the right financial habits, one needs to keep setting short-term goals and make sure to stick with your budget plans. Do not forget to reward yourself for reaching a certain goal: for example, you have successfully achieved the goal you have set for groceries, go treat yourself with a good dinner at a restaurant. You cannot cut down on your fixed bills but make sure to look for online deals or sales for shopping, memberships, etc. This practice may get you some good deals and also save you a lot of money.

Use a budget worksheet to keep everything organized. You can categorically track where you are spending more and where you can cut down on spendings. If you stray from your budget, it certainly means you are overspending. The budget sheet will help you identify the areas of concern. There are various ways one might overspend; understanding the category where you overspent will help you control it and keep your goals on track.

It is not advisable to keep "plastic money" (i.e. credit and debit cards), but in today's fast-moving world, having plastic money is more convenient than carrying cash everywhere. While using plastic money, a little research may help a lot. Be mindful of the interest rate that the banks charge on the credit card and the annual maintenance charges. Most of the banks offer loyalty points on their credit cards. These can be reimbursed for vouchers that can be used for shopping, cashback, etc. In some cases, if you pay the amount spent on the credit card before the statement is generated, you can avoid being charged interest on credit card usage. If possible, do not use credit cards for a while; the ease of buying anything online via credit/debit cards often results in buying things that we may not need and results in overspending. One might opt for old traditional ways of spending money using cash. This may not be a fast way but it has its benefits. When you use cash to buy products and services, you will be mindful of your spending and will be amazed to see how much you have saved.

Always plan, be it engagement, marriage, or starting a family, because it is not easy on your finances. Work on your time-line backwards to see how much you need to save every month to make that event happen smoothly.

Married couples can combine their finances, but always be transparent and accountable towards your finances and budget. Just like an alternate account, start a joint account, put your savings and emergency funds there, and operate a single spending account to have maximum clarity and to track your spendings. As a couple, make sure to discuss your budget and financial goals often, as sharing the same vision will make it easy for you to achieve goals. Do not forget to have a fun time together—go out for movies and dinners—but make sure you don't spend more than the allocated budget.

Save before you shop for anything like a motorbike or car. Do not hesitate to buy a used vehicle but ensure to get it checked thoroughly by the experts. Research well and negotiate well as this will help to make a good deal. Alternatively, you can always use public transportation as it will not only save your time but you will also save money on car insurance, fuel, and also reduce your carbon footprint.

Never forget the taxes. They are painful to pay but can be worse if not paid. Have a good accountant by your side and determine how much taxes need to be paid and allocate funds accordingly in your budget. Plan for the future, and keep your taxes ready in advance for the coming months or quarters.

Constantly review your budget as it may fluctuate each month; some months the bills may be high, some may be low. Review and adjust your budget to maximize your savings. Your budget will always play a great role in your life no matter at what point in your life you are. It is the first line of defense and highway towards your financial freedom. Plan it well and stick to it.

LIVING WITHIN YOUR MEANS

This mantra is the easiest way to live a stress-free life. It simply means that you spend less than what you earn. It is easier said than done for some people. In the age of instant money, where you have companies offering you instant credit cards and personal loans, it is easy to go off the track and start spending recklessly. But unfortunately, this behaviour is not sustainable. It is important to learn how to live within your means to understand your monthly income and budget your expenses in such a way that it allows you to achieve financial freedom.

Understand how much you make because that is your means to live. Most of our bills follow a monthly cycle. If you get paid weekly or biweekly, multiply the paychecks accordingly and get your monthly income. This will help you to create a proper budget. Plan your expenses and keep them less than what you earn. Most of us follow the principle of spending first and then whatever amount is left goes into savings. I would advise you to do the reverse. As soon as you receive your salary, keep aside a certain percentage of your money for savings. You can make it automatic, so that you will stop relying on that money. Whatever amount that is pending is now your expenses. If you want to increase your savings, then you can increase the percentage of the savings and use the remaining amount for your expenses. This approach will automatically result in living within your means ("Living Within Your Means," n.d.).

As I have said earlier, avoid using credit cards. They do not count towards your means. Most of the time, people are not able to keep up with the payments, which means that they end up paying a huge amount of interest. Also, the companies can stop your credit card any time, so definitely you cannot rely on credit cards. In case you want to purchase something, maybe a new sofa, save money for it. You cannot buy it on a credit card as that will defeat your purpose.

Apart from your savings, set up an emergency fund. You can start by adding $100 to $200 every month into a separate account for minor emergencies. Ideally you should keep up to six months of your salary as your emergency fund. You can also think of ways to increase your income. You can ask your company for a raise or take up a new job.

In the end, living within your means boils down to tracking your expenditures and spending your money wisely.

NON-DISCRETIONARY AND DISCRETIONARY EXPENSES

Non-discretionary expenses are mandatory expenses which include bills like groceries, taxes, rents, and other fixed expenses. They are usually defined as basic needs, something which you cannot live without. On the other hand, discretionary expenses are expenses which you can survive without. These are nothing but non-essential expenditures. Vacations and restaurant meals are some non-discretionary expenses.

While creating a budget, start with your non-discretionary expenses. Most of these expenses are fixed and if not paid for, the household will stop functioning. It is your discretionary expenses that can be adjusted depending on your financial condition. You can also rank your discretionary expenses in terms of their importance. This way, you will know which items need to be struck out of your budget during a financial crisis.

You can follow the 50-30-20 rule for your budgeting, which states that, "50% of your income should be allocated for essential expenses; 30% for non-essential expenses and 20% for your savings" (Rakoczy, n.d.).

INCOME AND TAXES

Income tax is the kind of tax that the government applies on individuals' and businesses' income. It utilises this tax to fund various programs for public service, development programs, and goods for the citizens and other reasons. It is important to understand the basics of the taxation system so that you can plan your budget accordingly.

Payroll Taxes

The federal government deducts payroll taxes before the salary is credited in an individual's account. In the US, the government uses this amount to fund Social Security and Medicare. These taxes are also called FICA taxes as they are mandated by the Federal Insurance Contributions Act. A significant portion, amounting to 6.20 percent of all the dollars earned up to an established limit, goes to Social Security (also called Old Age and Survivors Disability, OASDI), and 1.45 percent of all dollars earned, irrespective of your earnings, goes to The Medicare. So, your FICA tax will be 7.65 percent of your entire income unless your earnings share is more than the Social Security limit (Guthrie & Nicholls, 2015).

Federal Income Tax

Apart from the payroll taxes, there is an income tax levied by the federal government. The federal government taxation system is progressive, and the higher level of income will have a higher level of tax rate. The federal government also offers certain exemptions and deductions to reduce the tax load. There are certain amounts which are not counted under taxable income. For example, if you are contributing to a qualified retirement plan, it will not be taxed. Then there are certain exemptions, deductions, and credits, which also reduce the taxable income. These deductions are for health-care expenses, education expenses, and certain investments.

Low to middle income individuals qualify for some tax credits, which helps reduce the tax owed. Apart from the personal exemption, the government also provides standard deduction. Your tax filing status, i.e. your family or marriage status, influences your standard deduction.

State Income Tax

Apart from the federal tax, some states also impose state tax. Alaska, Florida, Nevada, New Hampshire, South Dakota, Tennessee, Texas, Washington, and Wyoming are the nine states that do not impose any state income tax on earned income. However, New Hampshire and Tennessee levy tax on income generated by your investments. Some states have progressive taxation system or they follow a flat rate system irrespective of your income levels. Some cities and counties also impose tax (Blokhin, 2019).

INCOME VS EXPENSES

One should try to pay attention to their income and expenses, and aim to be in the positive cash flow model. Spending money may give you instant gratification, but we need to understand the difference between want and need. We often end up spending more than we need. This approach often leads to high credit card bills, and most of the time, one tends to ignore the debt as the negative numbers always make us feel bad (Mastery, n.d.).

To maintain a positive cash flow, one must pay attention to the income and expenses. You may start by simply noting them down on a spreadsheet, Excel document, or even a blank piece of paper. Have a good look at your credit card bills, bank statements, and identify all the sources of income like salary or any passive mode of income. Then consider all the expenses like house rent, EMIs, bills, taxes, insurances, groceries, etc. Prioritize your expenses in terms of needs and wants. If you use a credit card, ensure to make your payments on time to avoid paying interest charges and late payment fees. This approach will help to build your credit score. A good credit score will help you in the future if you wish to take a loan to start a new business, get a mortgage, or fund further academic studies. To maintain or increase your positive cash flow, you can either look for a higher paying job or invest in passive income like business, stocks, and bonds. These investment options take time to show results, so the fastest way to increase your positive cash flow is to decrease your expenses. For example, taking public transport to work can be a better option than travelling by car, as you may save time, fuel, and a decent amount of money every month.

Prioritizing your expenses will always make your life easier. One can follow a few easy steps as described below.

You can invest 55% of your income into necessities that might include your house rent, groceries, internet/mobile bills, credit card bills, and utilities. You may aim to save 10% of your income towards long-term savings that may include your retirement planning or medical emergency. Invest another 10% in financial education and upskill yourself in handling the financial aspects of your life. Get a mentor, attend seminars, and learn how to invest money to generate passive income. This investment will help you in the long run to maintain positive cash flow. Another 10% of your income can go towards building an emergency fund that will allow you financial freedom. Invest this money into buying stocks and shares, bonds, and real estate. This investment is where your financial education will play an important role. Both education and investment plans will not just help you earn some extra cash but might also pull you out of debt. Investing in education will help you learn about finances and investment tricks. Hence, it will equip you to make the correct investment both long and short term, ensuring a regular positive cash flow.

Do not forget to reward yourself for all the planning and hard work you do, so keep another 10% for fun. Utilize this fund to socialize with friends and family, go out for dinners, go to movies, or shop for yourself. Make sure you stick to your plan and do not overspend. Keep five percent of your income for buying gifts, as giving is important. It is a kind of therapy that gives you a sense of abundance and is a feel-good factor. Also, this aspect will let others know that you are doing well in your life.

Being aware of your money will help you take control of your life, so budgeting becomes a good habit that makes you stress-free and financially secure.

Sticking to the budget that you have created is the most difficult step in budgeting. Many of us create a budget with good intentions, we follow it for a while, but we lack the good discipline to follow it long term, and hence we lose control over our budget. It is often considered that personal budgeting means applying restrictions on spending but in reality, you simply have to keep a track of your monthly expenses to make your budget effective. To have a good budget, one must be clear on their financial goals. Learn to live within your means. That simply means not to spend more than you earn, and to keep yourself out of debt.

Focusing on having a good credit score is a parameter to measure your financial health. One must aim to have a credit score above 800 as it helps you get easy loans. The higher the credit score, the lesser the interest rate applied on your loan, resulting in lower monthly payments against the loan. To reach a good credit score, we do not need to take any extraordinary steps. We should aim to pay our monthly bills on time, avoid any late payments, and take out personal loans only when there is a real need. These steps will help to avoid any interest being levied on the credit card and also the late payment fees. Prepare an emergency fund that will help you in any medical emergency or will be helpful if you lose your job in a recession. A good budget will allow you to lead a comfortable and happy life.

Senator Elizabeth Warren (a Harvard law professor when she coined the term) and her daughter, Amelia Warren Tyagi, in the book *All Your Worth: The Ultimate Lifetime Money Plan*, popularized the 50/30/20 rule of thumb for budgets (Vansomeren, 2011). This way one can allocate your funds in three categories: needs, wants, and financial goals. Before you apply this rule, you must understand how it works and also its limitations, as it is just an idea to plan your budget but it will not track your budget.

- 50% will include your rent, groceries, and utilities (electricity, water, phone bills, etc).
- 30% will include things that you desire and not that you need, like vacations, hobbies, dining out, subscriptions to Netflix, cable TV, etc.

- 20% goes towards your financial goals such as savings, investment, or debt payment.

To follow the 50/30/20 rule, follow the below steps:

- Calculate your monthly income, including your salary, interests, and any other sources of income. Subtract the estimated income taxes from your sum total. In case your employer is providing you a 401(k) benefit, you may want to match the contribution, so reduce that component from your take-home income.
- Jot down the expenses and divide them into two categories: needs and wants. The expenses without which your household will stop functioning will come under needs and the expenses which will alleviate your lifestyle are wants.
- Allocate your monthly income against each category of expense and also allocate 20% for your savings, which also includes your emergency fund.
- Track your expenses, and make changes where necessary if you are exceeding the threshold.

This rule usually works because managing finances can be a bit confusing and intimidating, but this simple rule helps allocate funds easily towards your monthly budget. You can begin with this simple rule, but remember to graduate with your budget and its tracking as this rule might have some grey areas as well, and it might be a bit difficult to categorize your spending in these three categories. For example, some groceries might fall in the category of "want," like an unhealthy snack, junk food, sodas, or alcoholic beverages.

Also, 20% of savings might not be enough, especially if you have big plans for the future like buying a house or starting a business. This rule might be helpful to start with, but make sure to keep educating yourself on finance and budgeting and move to a better plan to plan your finances.

Steps to Make Personal Budget

Until now, we have learned the personal budget is a means to balance your income and expenses, and in turn, can help you achieve your long term financial goals. It is a simple way to refrain from overspending and also keep your finances in the black. Before starting to create a budget, you should first decide the mode you want to use: it can be a simple excel sheet or a budgeting app.

Here are a few simple steps you can follow to create your budget:

- Get all your financial documents on the table, including:
- Pay slips
- Rent receipts
- Utility bills
- Investment details
- Any mortgage-related documents
- Credit card bills

Any other document which is either related to income or expense. These documents will help us to determine our monthly average.

- Compute your **total income**. If you have regular

paychecks, then your take-home salary will be regular income. Apart from this, also add if you have interest coming in regularly from your investments, or have some kind of financial aid being provided regularly. For freelancers, your lowest income in any given month can be the base of your budget.

- On the expenses side, create two sub-categories: non-discretionary (fixed) and discretionary (variable).
- Under your fixed expenses, add items without which the household will stop functioning. This may include rents, mortgage, utility bills, deposits to savings accounts, emergency funds, insurance premiums, and credit card bills. Sum up the total and deduct it from your income. The amount left can be used for variable expenses.
- Then list your variable expenses including restaurant bills, fitness classes, clothes shopping, and other expenses that are not a fixed one. This will give you a rough estimate of your spending habits.
- Add up your income and expenses. If the total of your fixed and variable expenses is more than the income, that means you are living above your means and your variable expenses need to be adjusted. If your income is more than your expenses, that is good as you are positive. You can save this for the future or use it to pay off some debt.
- Adjust your expenses to ensure that you achieve your long term financial goals. Adjusting your variable expenses is easier compared to fixed income. For variable expenses, you may cancel your gym membership or reduce the number of restaurant

meals. In case of your fixed income, you may adjust your electricity bills by adjusting your thermostats, or if you are paying higher rent, you can move to a place with lower rent.

We now know how to create the budget. Here are a few strategies that will help you to use your budget properly:

- The 50/30/20 rule: We have already learned in detail about this rule where 50% accounts for your needs, 30% for wants, and 20% for your savings.
- Zero-based budgeting is a way of budgeting where the net money left in your budget (not your account) after deducting expenses from your income is zero. Basically, each dollar in your income is accounted for by some expense. Every kind of emergency or possible bill should be accounted for. At the end of the exercise, if you still have some money pending, you can add it to your savings or pay off your credit card bill. The logic is if you have a few dollars pending and you have allocated it to a category, it will obviously be spent somewhere but you would not know where it has been spent. This will nullify the purpose of creating a budget.
- There is another strategy called the envelope system. It is somewhat similar to zero-based budgeting. It is more of a traditional approach as you use cash to manage your expenses. Basically, at the start of the month, you create separate envelopes for different categories of expenses that you have created. Each envelope will have cash and a name of the category written on it. If the money in the envelope is over,

this means you cannot spend any more money on that category.

Apart from these strategies, here are a few more tips to help you in this journey:

- If you are paid only once a month, then divide it into a weekly basis and use another to keep the additional cash for remaining weeks.
- Evaluate your budget at the end of the month, so that you can add any additional expense that was not accounted for. Tweak your budget if needed.
- Automate payments for important expenses like rent, savings, retirement funds, and mortgages so that you do not leave out these expenses by mistake. Keep an eye on the automated payments from time to time to ensure you are not overcharged at any given point of time.
- Use a credit card only if you will have money to pay off the bill at the end of the month. You do not want to spend on paying for huge credit card interest.
- Spend money to upskill yourself in financial literacy so that you can make your money earn for you. Check out the various investment tools which can help you in this process.
- In case you have to make cuts in some variable expense category, do not make it suddenly and all at once, as it is not sustainable. Instead, make small and gradual changes, so that your budget has the time to absorb the difference.

Your budget is not a line set in stone. Circumstances change and your wants may become needs or vice versa. Every few months, sit down and review your budget. Make necessary changes and ensure that your long term financial goals are met. Remember to make your budget work for you.

DEBT MANAGEMENT

*A*t times, people have to take on debts for various reasons. Debt management is about managing your debts. Usually, secured loans like mortgages and car loans do not fall under this category. You can hire an expert or try to manage them on your own. First, list your debts starting from lowest to highest. Then aim to clear off your smaller debts as this will give you a psychological boost that you can clear off your debts. Then for the bigger debts, either negotiate with your creditor to break it down to monthly payments, reduce the interest rate, or in the case of credit cards, check if you can transfer them to another card with lower interest rates. In the next few sections, we will understand the debt psychology and how to manage debt, as well as the details about credit score and how to get out of debt.

THE CONSUMER DEBT PSYCHOLOGY

There are several factors that drive debt behavior. There are three types of debtors: Non-debtors are people who do not owe any money to any company, mild-debtors at times delay their payments, and serious-debtors are people who have been sued by the creditors. Apart from economic and demographic factors, psychological factors play a vital role in driving consumer behavior in the case of serious debtors. A study was conducted to understand the psychological factors and we will discuss the same here.

Easy Acceptance of Debt by Society

The attitude of modern society towards debt has become more acceptable compared to earlier times. Debt is no longer seen as taboo but somehow, a culture has been developed that allows this attitude to flourish. It has been observed that serious-debtors prefer to live in a society where debt is more common and acceptable compared to non-debtors.

Family Culture Towards Debt

Debt is more prevalent for people where there has been a history of borrowing money in their families. Such individuals develop a higher tolerance towards borrowing money. If the parents had a successful history with debt, one is likely to get influenced, and follow on the same pathway.

Comparative Attitude

This attitude comes from the company you keep. If one tends to refer to people with higher economic sources to fund their rich lifestyle, that person is bound to get in the vicious trap of debt. There is a term for this kind of attitude: It is called "Keeping up with the Joneses." This kind of attitude is more status-driven and the person stops following any logical behavior. Most of the time, people don't realize they are depicting such behavior unless it is too late; instead they run away from reality. They are big spenders and believe in showcasing their wealth.

Money Management Styles

Managing your money properly defines the base of a good budget and will help one to lead a comfortable life. But unfortunately in the case of debtors, they lack the basic skills to manage their income and expenses. A non-debtor would usually prefer to save money to fulfill their wants instead of taking a loan or using a credit card. On the other hand, debtors will take a loan even if they have savings in hand. They fail to realise the amount of interest they will have to pay to fund this want. Serious debtors have been found to have weak money management styles. They tend to have low financial knowledge and a vague understanding of how they got into debt. They mostly do not invest in bonds and share markets. They tend to avoid discussion about money and keep no track of where their money is being spent. They have a tendency to overspend and end up in debt. They live with an attitude of living in the present and spending all the money they have.

Buying Patterns

Inappropriate buying patterns can affect your budget badly and make it fail in an epic way. People get into financial crises as they are not able to differentiate between wants and needs. Normally, what people deem as luxurious products, they deem as necessity and end up buying the items or services. This behavior is linked to having a comparative attitude too. They would buy expensive items for themselves or for their children especially during festivals and holidays. They start comparing themselves to others and think that what everyone buys will be important and necessary. This behavior is seen in comparison to their reference group. People with this kind of attitude are unable to say no to their kids and in return, fail to teach the importance of money to their children.

Time Horizons

Normally, in ideal situations, people take the future into consideration while making their spending decisions. They would increase their consumption both in quality and quantity over time. Some people face budget constraints and hence cannot increase their spending capacity. But at times, people ignore this constraint and borrow money to support their purchasing habits. They are less likely to save and spend more.

Sense of Control Over External Events

Did you predict that we would be hit by a pandemic or can you predict if you will keep your job? No, you cannot predict those things because these are external factors over which you have zero control. But there are some people who tend to believe that they have strong control over external events. This sense of control is also called "locus of control." People with a higher sense of this control are more likely to be in debt. "People with a strongly external locus of control were more likely to get into debt. Since debt is associated with poverty, and poorer people tend to give external reasons for economic phenomena such as poverty and unemployment, causality may run the other way. In either case, however, there should be a positive correlation between external locus of control and debt" (Lea et al., 1995).

DEBTORS VS NON-DEBTOR

Any person or company who owes money becomes a debtor. If one fails to make repayments on time, they will face huge penalties, high interest rates, and a drop in their credit score. Anyone who pays for the service or the product is not considered a debtor. We have the various factors that drive the behaviour of a debtor. In a study, the researchers spoke about the sociological factors that differentiate the debtors from the non-debtors. They spoke about factors like attitude towards money, life events, perceived control over finances, and other factors that affect the behaviour. We will understand the key behavioural differences between a debtor and a non-debtor (Livingstone & Lunt, 1992).

It was observed that families with more children were seen to have less debt problems, as they have to be more conservative and live on a fixed budget with minimum room for additional charges. Also, since their demands were more predictive and constant, they would try to avoid taking debts.

People in debt have less savings compared to those who do not have any debt. This difference indicates that debtors tend to spend more compared to saving. This attitude increases their debt. Another possibility is that debtors have usually utilised their entire savings and that is why they resort to taking more debt.

The other major difference is debtors think that loans and credit cards are a necessity in modern budgeting. They would satisfy not only their needs but also their wants, and take more debt. On the other hand, non-debtors view debt with disdain and would make all the efforts to avoid taking on debt. They follow the approach of saving enough money to satisfy their needs and wants. In case they are falling short of money, they would rather delay their wants than taking a loan or using a credit card.

Debtors and non-debtors also differ in their budgeting strategy. Debtors tend to lack self-control and have a flexible budget. They would change depending on the choice and demands. Non-debtors have a fairly detailed budget and they make every effort to stick to it under any circumstance. Keeping a flexible approach will push you in the direction of loans and hence losing control over your budget.

Another important difference is people who borrow more frequently tend to enjoy shopping more, as they believe in giving gifts and bribes. They discuss money in their social circle, but the discussion is more related to lack of money that can help them buy certain services and products to improve their lifestyle. They are generally more dissatisfied with their standard of living. On the other hand, non-debtors do not resort to bribery or gifting. They are more content in their lives and find less pleasure in materialistic things.

WHAT LEADS TO MORE DEBT

There has been a marked increase in the consumer credit and personal loan segment. No longer is taking a loan or using a credit card frowned upon. People have bought houses but have not been able to keep up with the installments, with the end result being that the house is repossessed by the creditor. Using credit cards to sustain your current lifestyle with bills piling on has become quite common. Yet there is a section of the population who have managed their budget properly, have a decent credit score, and manage to clear their debt on time. What drives this difference in the behavior of the consumers and what leads to increasing the amount of the debt? We will aim to address these questions in this section.

We have seen why people get into debt; we will now look into some reasons why some people get deep into debt and may have to file for bankruptcy.

Medical expenses are one of the biggest reasons why people land into debt. If someone is suffering from a rare or serious illness, it may result in bills worth thousands of dollars. In some cases, in spite of a job and health insurance, clearing off these bills requires people to use their savings, and take debt to clear these bills. Once all these resources have been exhausted, filing for bankruptcy may appear as the only option left.

Losing a job can put your finances under a lot of stress. Especially during the recent pandemic, many people lost their jobs owing to prolonged lockdown in many states. At times, people were not given severance packages, and ended up using their savings. The situation may become worse if one doesn't have an emergency fund. Using credit cards to keep the boat afloat will increase the debt load. In an unfortunate situation, if people are unable to find a job over a prolonged period, they may find it difficult to make the repayment on time, and ultimately get deep into debt.

Poor money management skills and high credit usage to maintain a certain lifestyle will make it difficult for someone to live within their means. Some people cannot hold themselves back from spending. They will buy everything on installments and credit cards, and ultimately, this spending gets out of their hands and they are not able to pay even the minimum due amount. This category of people feel a sense of entitlement wherein they think they are supposed to have everything their friends have or celebrate even a small accomplishment, even if they are not able to afford it. This not only affects their credit score but pushes them towards the brink of filing for bankruptcy.

Domestic issues like divorce and separation can put a tremendous strain on both parties involved. There is a huge legal fee involved, then the divorce clauses items, like paying alimony, division of marital assets, and child support, can further make the situation difficult. In cases, the spouses fail to pay the alimony, and the other party has to resort to using credit cards and taking loans.

Natural causes like earthquakes, tornadoes, or fire can damage property or destroy them completely in some cases. If houses are not insured against these calamities, they will be forced towards bankruptcy. So, they are not only stripped from their possessions but also their homes. Most house owners are not aware about catastrophe insurance, which provides them protection against these natural disasters and also some man-made disasters like terrorist attacks or riots.

In some cases, the debt starts when they start their lives as students. With the rising tuition costs, it has become inevitable for students to take loans to fund their graduate or postgraduate studies. This results in one accumulating debt even before the income has been made to make the payment (Smith, 2019).

In order to meet their daily needs while being a student, one has to either rely on credit cards or personal loans if their parents are not in the position to fund their kids' studies. By the time you finish your schooling, you already have accumulated a lot of debt on your personal sheet along with huge interest.

From there, you may need to take an auto loan to help you commute to your workplace. You visit the showroom, buy the car on installments, and along with a car (the value of which depreciates over time and thus makes it a non-useful purchase), you would have added another payment to your account. Post this, once you are married you may want your own space. This means you will have to take a home mortgage and add the home installment payment to the increasing order of debt. In case your income is increasing, managing these debts is possible if you manage your money properly. But in case you are stuck with the same salary, you may find it difficult to pay the huge debt.

With increasing debt, your ability to get a loan at a lower interest rate reduces, and hence, you will have to pay a large amount of interest. High interest loans, limited pay, and credit card payments will affect your money flow. This way, you end up in a vicious debt cycle where you will borrow to fulfill your needs and wants. All this inconsistency in repayments and frequent borrowing may push you to file for bankruptcy.

Debt can limit your life both physically and mentally. According to a study, 66% reported that due to loan burden that they were unable to save money, which will help in the future, (Staff, 2019). Not all debt is bad; if you have taken a loan to upgrade your skills or buy a house, these investments will help you in the future. The problem arises when you are unable to keep up with regular payments and the bills keep piling up. There are many ways one can get out of the debt situation, some of which will be discussed in the next section.

TIPS FOR MANAGING DEBT

We have so far learned about the various circumstances and behavior that drive an individual to borrow money. The thing to note here is that debts are not always bad. If the debt helps you to earn money in the future, it is considered to be good debt. For example, if you take out a mortgage to buy a property or shares, that may grow in value in the future and will make you money when you sell it.

On the other hand, bad debt is of no economic value. It will not help to make any money in the future. This includes buying branded clothes, going on vacations, and purchasing other items deemed as luxurious or non-essential.

Here are some debt management tips that will help you to manage your money better and support you in saving and building your future:

- Make a consolidated list of your debts. Include details like the amount, interest rate, creditor details, late payment fees, due date, and monthly instalments. This consolidation will help to create a big picture and understand your debts better. This will serve as an eye-opener for you. Calculate your debt-to-income ratio; that is, divide your debt with your income. The lower the ratio, the better financial situation you are in.

- Now add your income and other regular expenses. This will help you understand your current situation in terms of your income, and money that is left after spending on buying the essentials. See if there is a room to reduce the money on essentials and any room that will help to pay off your debts.

- Check if you can consolidate all your debts under one umbrella. This will help to reduce the number of interest and late payment fees. Managing a single loan payment will be easier than juggling several payments. But be mindful of following the payment schedule, as any further delays will result in paying more to the lender.

- If you have loans from multiple sources, then decide on which bill should be paid first. My suggestion would be to first pay the credit card bills, as normally, they have a high rate of interest and can add a major chunk to your outstanding.

- Create a cycle to pay your debt payments monthly. Use a payment calendar and mark your paycheck dates, and then accordingly, mark the dates where you will make the payments. You can also set up alerts on your phone or make a facility for automatic payments to clear the debt. This planning will help you to avoid any misses, late payment charges, and hefty interest charges. Late payments also affect your credit score, which eventually affects your ability to borrow money.

- One should aim to clear the outstanding bills completely instead of paying only the minimum required amount. If you pay only the minimum amount, then the interest will be levied on the remaining amount, adding up your outstanding amount. But in case you do not have the money, then clear the minimum amount, as that will help you avoid the late payment fees. Missing your payments will make it harder for you to catch up and could ultimately tag you as a defaulter.
- Tweak your budget a bit, and see if you can make some extra repayments in a given month. This extra payment will help you to clear off your bills quickly and reduce the amount of interest accrued. Before doing this, check with your lenders to make sure there are no prepayment charges, as that will nullify your purpose.
- Set up a contingency plan in case you are let go from your job or some unexpected payment comes up which will delay your debt repayment.
- Reach out for help if you think that you are not able to manage your money well. There are many credit counseling agencies that offer help in getting your bills and savings sorted.

Now that we have some tips handy to manage your debt well, we will now look into the importance of credit score and how to improve it (Irby, 2011).

CREDIT SCORE AND HOW TO IMPROVE IT

Credit score is a number that defines one's credit worthiness. It falls in the range of 300 to 850. A credit score above 700 is usually considered good and above 800 is considered excellent. The main goal of any credit scoring system is to tell the lenders how risky it may be to do business with you. The higher the credit score, the more likely you are to make your repayments on time and less risky to do business with you. A higher credit score will not only improve your chances of getting the loan, but also improve the chances of getting the loan at lower interest rates. Over time, even a small difference in the interest rate, can make substantial savings on the interest. Thus, it is advisable to have a good credit score. On the other hand, a lower credit score will reduce your credit worthiness.

Credit score is calculated based on your credit history, total debt, open accounts, repayment history, and other items. Based on your credit score, the lenders decide if you will make your payment in a timely manner in future.

The credit score is the starting point; the lenders may have their own rating mechanism and rules to evaluate the consumer for loans or issuing credit cards. They may use your employment history, proof of income, and other factors before deciding on lending the money along with the rate of interest. They also take the external events into consideration and try to gauge how a consumer will get impacted with these events. The commonly used credit-scoring systems are FICO and VantageScore.

Fair Isaac Corporation, or FICO, developed the FICO credit score model. It is used by many financial institutions. It creates different types of credit scores. There is a base FICO score and industry-specific score. Base FICO scores can be used across multiple industries; on the other hand, industry-specific scores are used by auto lenders and credit card issuing companies.

- Any lender can use base FICO scores. The probability of a customer falling behind on any repayment can be determined by these scores. They range from 300 to 850.
- Auto lenders and credit card issuers use industry-specific FICO scores. They are called auto scores and bankcard scores. Again, the probability of any consumer to fall behind on a specific type of account can be determined by these scores. They range from 250 to 900.

VantageScore is another scoring model that skims through the information about your credit history and assigns a value to highlight the probability of you following a payment system completely. The excellent score range is from 750 to 850, and anything from 650 to 750 is considered to be good.

Here are a few common factors that affect your credit score ("What Affects Your Credit Scores?", 2017).

- Payment history is one of the most important factors in determining your credit score. On-time repayments will help in the long run to maintain a good credit score. Pay the minimum due amount to continue to be in the good books. Missing even one payment can impact your credit score negatively. Lenders want to check that you will follow the payment schedule. Your score could also be impacted by having an account sent to collections or filing bankruptcy.

- The duration of the credit history is also another important factor. This contains your newest account, oldest account, and the average of all the accounts. The longer the history, the better credit score you will have.

- The amount that you owe also affects your credit score. The amount that you owe, number of owned accounts, and percentage of the credit limit being used on revolving accounts together contribute to this factor. It is recommended not to use more than 30% of the available credit limit.

- Credit mix or different types of credit accounts affect your credit score. This credit mix includes installment accounts and revolving accounts. When you take a loan for a fixed amount and you pay a fixed amount along with interest every month, it becomes installment credit. Examples include home loans, student loans, and personal loans. In revolving credit, you get a credit limit and you have to pay a minimum due amount, depending on the limit that you have utilized. Credit cards are an example of revolving credit. Handling both the credits well will benefit your scores.

- Opening new credit accounts or you have made some credit enquiries affects your credit score. Having too many accounts or having made a lot of enquiries will increase your risk and in turn affect your score negatively.

We will now look at how FICO and VantageScore score the factors ("What Is a Good Credit Score?", 2019).

FICO uses percentage to state the importance of each factor.

- Payment history: 35%
- Amounts owed: 30%
- Length of credit history: 15%
- Credit mix: 10%
- New credit: 10%

VantageScore grades them based on how influential the factors are.

- Total credit usage, balance, and available credit: Extremely influential
- Credit mix and experience: Highly influential
- Payment history: Moderately influential
- Age of credit history: Less influential
- New accounts opened: Less influential

There are certain factors that both the agencies do not consider while determining the credit score ("What Is a Good Credit Score?", 2019).

- The US law prohibits agencies from using race, colour, marital status, sex, national origin or religion to influence your rating
- Age and your address

- Your salary and employment history
- Soft enquiries made by promotional companies or when you check your score

Tips to Improve Your Credit Score

- Make your payments on time and the minimum due amount if you are not able to pay the entire payment. Do not miss your payments under any circumstances. In case you think you will be missing your installment, talk to the creditor and check if some option for hardship can be worked out.
- Credit utilisation rate compares your current balance and the credit limit allocated by the creditor in case of revolving accounts. Always aim to keep your credit utilisation rate low, ideally in single digits.
- If you have a credit card and you are not using it, then keep it. Do not close the account as closing your account will impact your credit score. This will help to keep your credit utilisation rate low.
- Open credit accounts that will add to your credit report and will in turn be visible to credit rating agencies. These accounts can be installment accounts like education loans, car loans, and others, or revolving accounts like your credit cards.
- Apply for a credit only when you need it, as this request will lead to hard enquiry. This enquiry may affect your credit score slightly.
- In case you do not have time or knowledge to improve your credit score, work with the experts. These credit repair companies will work on your

behalf, negotiate with lenders and credit rating agencies, and improve your credit score. They may charge some monthly fee but in the long run it would be beneficial as maintaining a good score comes with a lot of benefits.

We have seen that maintaining a good credit score can help you get loans at lower interest rates, which in turn helps you save a lot of money in the long run. There are multiple factors that affect your credit score and it is up to you to maintain a good score and be eligible for more lending options at a lower rate, if the need arises.

HOW TO GET OUT OF DEBT - LOANS AND MORTGAGES

According to a report, an average American owes approximately $92,727 in total debt. The debt includes mortgages, student loans, credit card bills, and some other personal loans (Beattie, n.d.). If you are deep into debt, you should make efforts to clear your debt. Having huge debt is not only detrimental for your budget, it is also bad for your mental and physical health. Stress related to money can make it difficult for you to work towards your future savings. When you are debt-free, your confidence level increases and makes you hopeful for the future.

Deciding to get out of debt is your first step in digging your way out of this hole. It is not an easy task, but it is doable if you put your mind to it and make some necessary financial changes. Here we will discuss some ways to get out of debt (Beattie, n.d.):

- Address your debt situation. Get all the bills, loan statements, credit card statements, and any other outstanding documents together. Create an Excel sheet and add each debt item in one column. Add your income from all the sources in the next column. This is your ground zero situation. Clearly define your non-discretionary and discretionary expenditures. If your non-discretionary expenses exceed your net-income, you may need to move to a smaller space or cut down on your utility bills.

- Create a plan by clearly defining the order you will be paying the debt. It may be a loan with the highest interest rate or the lowest amount first. Make a plan based on the priority. Also, ensure that while you are paying for one account, you should be paying the minimum amount in other outstanding bills, or else you may have to pay late payment charges.

- Do not make the mistake of taking more loans to clear off your other debts. You can keep your credit cards if you do not use them, but remember not to close the credit cards as that may affect your credit score. Learn to live within your means, as adding more debt will create more pressure on your monthly budget.

- Keep checking your budget on a monthly basis and see if you can reduce your spending in any category. Think twice before making any expense as this cautious approach will help you to clear your debt. Check if some frivolous spending in the past got you into this situation. A cautious approach will remind you not to fall in the debt trap again.

- Check out the possibility of increasing your income.

You can take up a second job, ask for a hike in your current salary, sell items that you do not require, do some freelance work, or take up odd jobs to add to your current income. This will help you as you would not need to use the credit card and also make some extra money to clear your debt.

- In case you are not able to manage your funds well, talk to a credit counsellor. They will provide useful tips, talk to your creditors, negotiate with them to reduce your interest rate, and take necessary steps to clear your debt. You have to be careful with the fees that they will charge for their services.
- Time will be of essence here as late payments will increase your financial burden. For example, if you do not pay in this month, next month you will have twice the amount to pay along with late payment fees, and also reduced credit rating.
- Do not get overwhelmed by the situation. Keep your calm and tackle one debt at a time. This one step at a time approach will make managing your debt more streamlined and doable. Keep a track of your progress and step by step, you will finish this marathon.

There are two strategies which are commonly used to clear the debt. They are debt avalanche and debt snowball methods (Kagan, n.d.).

- In the debt avalanche method, an individual pays the minimum due amount for all the outstanding bills and any remaining fund to the debt with the highest interest rate. Once the debt with the highest interest rate is paid off, then the next debt comes into the picture. This practice is followed till all the debt is cleared.

- This method helps to reduce the interest paid to a large extent and thereby the debt amount substantially. Most creditors use compound interest, which increases based on the frequency of the interest applied. Almost all the credit card companies apply interest on a daily basis, which leads to accumulation of a lot of debt. Thus, when you clear the debt based on the interest rate, you will reduce your debt to a large extent. But this method requires a lot of self-control and discipline. In case any unplanned expense comes up, your debt repayment plan can go for a toss. It is therefore recommended to create an emergency fund by saving for six months and then start on this path.

- In the snowball method also, one should pay the minimum due on the debts, but one should allocate funds to first clear the debt with lowest value, followed by the next larger debt. This method increases your confidence and gives you the much needed motivation that you can clear off the debt. Also, it is easy to implement as you just need to rank the debts in terms of their value and start paying. On the other hand, you will pay a lot of interest in this method as the debt with the highest interest rate still has a lot of money pending. This increase will increase the time required to clear the debts.

- Snowball method provides more mental peace than economical. The decrease in the number of items provides a gratification that will keep you motivated.

But in case you are on a time bound mission, the avalanche method works for you. Also, you will end up paying less in avalanche methods.

For some fortunate people, it may be possible that the smallest amount has the highest interest or the highest loan will have the lowest interest rate. In this case, you will be following both the methods. Whatever be your approach, you should aim to clear the debt and focus on saving. In the next chapter, we will talk about various benefits and instruments available to help you save and live a comfortable life in the long run.

THE ART OF SAVING

＊

*S*aving is a process where one keeps a certain portion of the income aside for future use. People may add small or big amounts to this pool regularly or as and when there is spare cash available. Over a period, a reasonable amount is accumulated which people may use for a pre-decided goal or as their retirement fund. According to a report (Rakoczy, n.d.), 20% of Americans have no retirement savings and 45% of Americans lack preparation in case their retirement savings run out. No economist has ever said that one should not save money. The importance of saving money was never negated by anyone. Still, there is a whole section of the population who have no savings and are doing nothing to improve the situation.

Apart from securing your retirement, saving money can give you the necessary financial flexibility. Instead of using a credit card or taking a loan to buy a house or any other household good, you can save money to buy that and in turn, save money on huge interest. Plus, savings can help you to fulfill your basic needs in case of any emergency like loss of job or a medical emergency.

Saving money also provides you financial security and makes your life easier. You will be able to maintain the same life-style if you have savings. You can also take calculated risks if you have a strong financial security. You can pursue your passion, open up a new café, or try new things if you have some savings kept aside.

But before we get into more details about how and why one should save money, we should understand why some people can save money or others believe in living in the present and spending money.

THE PSYCHOLOGY OF SPENDING AND SAVING

Our attitude towards money management most of the time is influenced by our upbringing. We often think that saving money is the right way to live and end up feeling guilty if we spend money. In reality, extreme behaviour of any kind is not advisable. There is no right or wrong way to deal with money, but it is about finding a balance between the two approaches.

A saver will save money thinking about the future. They are good with budgeting and can live within their means. They can live comfortably and are always looking for ways to stretch their money as much as possible. They are knowledgeable about the various saving schemes and can be patient when it comes to fulfilling their financial goals. But this behaviour also has a negative side. In extreme cases, savers find it difficult to part with their money and can become anxious when it comes to spending. Also, their behaviour can at times be seen as cheap and too rigid by others. They tend to forget that life is also about living and can delay gratification to an extent that they become irritated.

Let us try to understand why some people save. They save for various reasons like retirement, marriage, their children's education, a down payment for a house, or emergency situations like a medical emergency, or the loss of a job. They save because they feel that the future is uncertain and emergency funds are needed to help them get through with their living expenses. Savers tend to regret it if they are not able to save. They consider home mortgages as savings, as the value of a home tends to increase over time and also they aim to give their homes to their future children. There are many theories that state people are motivated to save for economic reasons, where they aim to use the money in future and can gain some interest. The other reason why people are motivated to save money is purely for social reasons. They have been brought up with the principle of saving and thus feel morally obligated to save (Argyle & Furnham, 2021/2013).

According to a theory, a person saves money with eight motives (Argyle & Furnham, 2021/2013):

- To save for an emergency situation.
- As a means to fulfill future demands, as the needs will differ with age and situation.
- To get more interest on the income.

- To improve the quality of life in the future and increase the rate of spending in the future.
- To become financially secure and independent so that one can do anything of their choice in the future.
- To save a lumpsum amount of money in order to start a business in the future.
- To be able to lend money to others in the future.
- To act like a pure miser and spend a minimum amount of money.

There is another theory (Argyle & Furnham, 2021/2013) that states that a person's habits and beliefs about savings depend on the reference group. If the people in the reference group tend to save a lot of money, the individual will also act likewise. But if the reference group believes in living in the moment and caters to the wants of the family, the individual will also spend a lot of money and believe in instant gratification (Argyle & Furnham, 2021/2013).

There is a theory (Argyle & Furnham, 2021/2013) that is related to age and economic condition of the individual. It has been observed that young people and people in old age can save more than middle-age people. Retired people tend to have less responsibility and so can save more. Middle aged people have children and they have to cater to their demands, thereby increasing their expenditure. Habitual savers see credit as a failure. They see it as an economic protection and are prone to take risks to increase their savings.

On the other hand, spenders believe in living their life to the fullest and living in the present. They are much more relaxed and use money as a means to fulfill their needs and wants too. They believe in instant gratification and end up buying things just because they want it. The downside of this behaviour is that they often end up in debt and find it difficult to get out of it. They become anxious when the budgeting gets out of hand and feel remorseful.

Spenders are seen to get affected by advertisements and lack self-control. Thus, they are more prone to using credit cards and taking personal loans to fit their lifestyle. They are careless with their budgeting and often rake up a lot of debt with zero savings. Spenders tend to be easily influenced by external factors and often blame themselves for overspending and do not seek any social support. Their budgeting strategy is flexible and lets the money control them. Unlike savers who buy from their favourite shops, spenders buy from multiple places (Argyle & Furnham, 2021/2013).

Money is meant to improve your life. Yes, it is important to save money but one should not forget to live life too by occasionally catering to the wants that improve your mental and physical health. The trick is to find that perfect balance where you are not bogged down with credit card bills and are not also not turning into an anxious Uncle Scrooge who is constantly thinking about money and forgets to live life.

HOW TO PROMOTE SAVING CULTURE

According to a report (Urosevic, 2020), 69% of Americans have less than $1,000 in their savings account and only 30% of Americans included savings as part of their financial planning. This figure is worrisome as the pandemic has taught us that living within our means and saving for the rainy days is important. We have seen that small business owners, people working as freelancers or on daily wages needed their savings to fulfill their basic needs.

- We have seen that saving is more of an attitude than an economical trait. There are plenty of cases where people with high income have very little savings and people with less money have managed to save a decent amount. There are many factors and ways to drive this behavior.
- People can upskill themselves by learning about the best way to manage their money and create that spare cash that can be counted as savings. This requires a more proactive approach to learn about money management on a day-to-day basis. They should aim to be more disciplined and organized in their financial dealings. Remind yourself to save money till it becomes a habit and comes naturally to you.
- Confront your negative attitude towards money management. Habits and attitudes can be changed. Occasional gratification is acceptable but do not let money drive you. If your friend circle is more inclined towards spending money, then consciously make efforts not to follow them. Reignite the passion and confidence that you can live within your means and at the same time save money for your goals and retirement.
- It is all about taking that first step in this journey. If

you are new on this journey, then start small, say no to that expensive coffee at the café and save your hard-earned money. Challenge yourself and make yourself believe that saving is possible and that no major sacrifices are required. Set short-term and realistic goals, identify the areas where you can easily make some cuts, and start saving while building your confidence. Slowly, this will not look like a task but the way to live.

- Planning to buy a sofa or buy a car or simply upgrade your wardrobe? Instead of reaching for your credit card to make payment, you can instead make a goal of saving for these objectives and use your savings to fulfill your wishes. This will save you money on interest and also encourage you to continue saving. Once the goals are achieved, you will feel more confident, and can create a cycle of success.

- Challenge yourself to learn new investment skills and make your money work for you. Do not look at saving as a chore, but instead, make it fun by joining some classes, and giving yourself some gratification if you have achieved a goal.

- In some countries, saving money is taught right from childhood. Kids are given a piggy bank where they have to save money till the piggy bank is full. Once the piggy bank is full, they can break open it and use it to buy an item of their choice. This habit continues with them during adulthood too and teaches them self-control. As I have said earlier, habits can be changed. So, in case you have been a spender so far, go ahead and buy your first piggy bank, start adding money to it, and form a healthy habit.

- Social validation goes a long way in helping you to stick to your target. Inform your friends and family about your new plan to save and ask for help to make you accountable to follow the plan. For example, if you fail to achieve your target savings for the month, you will pick up your friend's kids for a week. You can form a savings club and ensure that every month each member will add the agreed amount for a fixed period of time. With a larger group, each person will be accountable to keep the plan on track and ensure that the target is achieved.

- Every month set up a schedule with your bank to auto-debit a fixed amount to your savings account and ensure that you cannot remove any money from the account for a fixed period. In some cases, the bank also offers fixed term deposit interest rates. Check with your bank about this approach and follow it.

- There are many apps available in the market which are based on machine learning. You can feed in your income and regular expenses and also set up a target to save. Follow this practice for a few months, and the app will study your data, and create and understand your spending pattern. It will then identify areas when expenditures can be cut and instead divert them to your savings. Like impulsive shopping, there is a concept of impulsive saving where the app directly transfers the spare cash to the savings account.

- The average lifespan of an individual has increased

but the retirement age has remained constant. With the increase in lifespan, you cannot rely on a limited retirement fund to sustain once you have stopped working. You should also consider inflation rates and back calculate the amount of money you will require in the future to continue living a comfortable life. This calculation will push you to save more and live a decent life.

- In case you are not happy in your current job or you want to start a small business in the future, saving money can help you to make the transition. You may want to go to school later to upskill yourself so that you can change your field, so your savings will help to meet your basic needs. This dream of financial independence should encourage people to save money.

- If you suddenly start feeling demotivated to continue with your savings, remind yourself why you start saving in the first place. It may be to fund your kid's education or go on a dream vacation or buy a house in the future. Keep your end goal in mind while moving on in this journey. Maybe you have been saving for a while and have lost focus, but remind yourself of the reason. Maybe you love baking and want to start a new bakery or you want to move up the ladder in your corporate career but the lack of a post-graduation degree is holding you back. It may be for any reason, but go visit it, and get back on track with renewed enthusiasm.

HABITS OF SUCCESSFUL SAVERS

We live in an era where we have a plethora of credit cards and loan options available. One swipe and we get the desired product, but along with it comes the additional payment in the form of interest. Have you ever wondered how people used to buy things before credit cards became a norm? It is very simple—they used to save and buy things to satisfy their needs and wants. Habitual savers have more savings in their account and are less likely to use credit as a means to live. According to research in the UK, apart from age and income, there are certain personality traits that drive one to save on a regular basis ("The Three Habits of Successful Savers," 2014). In the next section, we will understand these personality traits.

Saving On a Monthly Basis

Regularly saving on a monthly basis will help to build a savings portfolio and maintain it. This regular approach is better than saving on a need basis as it will make a significant difference to your portfolio. I have already highlighted the different methods of savings. A successful saver every month parks aside a fixed amount of money for savings. The method of 50-30-20 comes into picture here. They pay themselves first before making any other payment. Wondering where to start to make this a habit?

- Auto-debit and employee savings plans: One can opt for an auto debit service where every month, a fixed amount is deposited in the savings account. In some countries, there are some government-run schemes where the individuals can create an auto-debit rule where the money is deposited in the savings account and a fixed interest can be earned on the savings. This money will be locked for a fixed period and the individual cannot withdraw money under any circumstances.

Apart from the pension scheme, there are many employee savings plans run by the employer that allows the employees to keep a certain portion of their income for retirement or other long term goals. In some cases, employers match the contribution of the employees. The savings schemes allow the employees to save taxes and build a corpus amount to fund their long-term requirements. The employees have to be employed with the employers for a certain period before they become eligible to utilize these schemes (Kagan, 2019b).

In the US, the most common employee savings plan is the 401(K) retirement plan. Employee savings plans can be of mainly two types: Defined contribution plans under which 401(K) comes, and schemes sponsored by public or non-profit companies. In both plans, the amount is auto-deducted before taxes are calculated. With increasing medical costs, there is another scheme that comes under employee savings plans. A Health Savings Account is a tool that helps to cover the medical expenses that are usually not covered by other medical plans (Kagan, 2019b).

- Use existing debt repayment amounts to instill a savings habit. It was observed in the research that some people cannot start with savings as they are clearing some debts. Lenders can work out a plan with the debtors to divert a certain percentage of

their debt repayment amount into the savings
account. This will help to clear the debt and also
have a small savings at the end of the debt period.

In another method, the lenders can come up with a product where once the debt is cleared, the debtor will have to continue with the same amount of payment to the creditors. The catch here is instead of debt repayment, the additional amount will be diverted to the savings account. Since the debtors are already forgoing a certain amount as a habit, it will be easier for them to let go of the same amount to build up some savings. After a certain period, the consumers will have an option to opt-out of the scheme.

Saving for Emergency

We have already read that for some people, savings lie very low in the priority list. They prefer to spend money and live in today than save money for the future. It is important to highlight the benefits of savings to this section of the population. Habitual savers enjoy better peace of mind, can manage their budget better, and are much better prepared for any eventuality.

For any saver, peace of mind and safety of their hard-earned money are two important factors that they consider before investing in any scheme. For them, these factors are more important than high returns. Also, there is a certain section of audience who think savings will cut down on the money available for the expenditure. In order to push this section to saving more, product designers can come up with certain incentives like free movie tickets or some additional free vouchers or discount coupons, which will seem like a compensation for the amount invested towards savings. These incentives can be stopped if the regular savings have stopped.

Habitual savers save six months of the earnings for emergency funds. They are focused towards securing their future, while making small adjustments in their present. They do not have any particular goal to save but they save for no particular reason. They believe in ear-marking a certain percentage of their amount on a monthly basis towards savings. They allow themselves to enjoy their lives time and again, but they ensure that the savings used for enjoyment is replenished again.

Keeping Your Savings Aside From Your Other Earnings

Habitual savers keep their savings separate from their current account. This step prevents them from using their savings account. To start with the habit of saving, one can open an account to save money to accomplish a particular goal. It can be to sponsor a vacation or buy a car, but this saving may not turn into a regular habit. To regularise this saving, one can lock away the amount into a savings account and a rule of regular deposits can be applied by the service owner. These cannot be accessed except in case of an emergency. The savings firm or banks can offer extra incentives that will promote people to keep the money in the savings account as opposed to using the amount.

Other Habits That Define Habitual Savers

Apart from these habits, successful savers practice better self-control and are more financially literate compared to other people. They are more optimistic about the future and tend to make their money work for them. Another important differentiating factor is the company they keep. Nick Holeman, a certified financial planner, said, "You are the average of the three people you spend the most time with," as reported in CNBC. He said that successful people have peers and friends that have similar mindset. Habitual savers have friends that value money, they save and invest money regularly and believe in living within their means. He also added that if you have friends who are always talking about living in the present and spending money, you should consider making a new circle of friends (Cornfield, 2020).

Building an emergency fund is important as a tragedy does not ask for permission before striking. Many people have lost their livelihood and had to file for bankruptcy as they could not save for the "what if" situations. You may feel disappointed if a new dress is not purchased immediately or if you were not able to join your friends for a beach vacation because you were saving money, but in the long run, you will have better peace of mind and obviously a better bank balance. Delaying your gratification for sometime can be difficult but it is worth the pain.

Also, savers may own a credit card but that is solely from the point of view of increasing their credit score. They ensure that any amount spent on credit cards is paid towards the end of the month, so that they do not have to pay any extra late payment fees or interest. They truly understand the importance and follow the practice of living below the means.

SIMPLE STEPS AND ACTIONS TO SAVE MONEY

- The success of your budget and ultimately your saving plan will be less dependent on your income but more dependent on your spending. Track your expenses and understand where your money is going. Keep a record of all the bills including your coffee bills, cash tip, and any other household item. Divide into discretionary and non-discretionary expenses. Remove any spending that is not required for your house to function.

- Account for your savings in your monthly budget planning. You can start off small with $100 a month. Understand the importance of the time factor when it comes to money. The longer time your money will have, the higher value it will grow. You may think that spending $50 on shoes will not make any difference, but even $50 in your savings account will increase in value over a few years. When you are saving for the long term, every penny counts. You have to find a way to save money every single day. Cut back on your grocery bills, reduce your entertainment expenditure by switching to cheaper cable plans, and look out for options when buying an insurance plan. Find a way to cut down your utility bills, and switch to a cheaper calling plan. Ensure that you allow yourself to have some fun once in a while, as you do not want to feel resentful and deprived. This feeling of resentment may backfire and get you off the savings track.

- To initially streamline your savings habit, create some short-term and long term goals. Decide on what you do want to achieve, understand how much money will be required, and start saving. Here are some examples of short-term and long-term goals.
- Short term goals can include building your emergency fund of six months living expenses, funds required to pay for your car down payment or fund your house renovation. Usually, short term goals are in the time-frame of one to three years.
- Long term goals can include building your retirement funds, starting a business, marriage, and funding your child's education. Long term goals are in the time-frame of more than four years.
- Educate yourself about the different saving options available in the market. These accounts are generally safe and give decent returns. Ideally you should spread your savings into different tools so that you can get maximum benefit (Lake, n.d.).
- Savings accounts are deposit accounts that can be opened at any bank or credit union. This account can be used for both short-term and long-term saving goals. They are safe and pay interest. It is on the lower side and as of May 2021, the average annual percentage yield (APY) of 0.07%.
- High-Yield Savings Accounts are offered by online banks and hence the returns are relatively higher than traditional savings accounts. As the overhead costs are less in the case of online banks, they can afford to pay more interest.
- You can open a money market account that offers a combination of savings account and checking

account. You can use this account for mid to long term goals. Once you have reached your goal, you can draw a check to fund your goal.

- Certificates of deposits, or CDs, are term deposits in which you can deposit your money for a pre-defined time frame. It can range from 30 days to 10 years, and you can earn interest on your deposit for the time-frame. Once the CD has matured, you can withdraw the initial amount along with the interest. However, please note that a penalty may be applied to some CDs in case you withdraw before it is matured.

- Individual Retirement Accounts, or IRAs, are specifically opened to fund your retirement goal. You have two options under this: traditional and Roth IRA. Under traditional IRA, you can get some tax benefit but there will be some tax levied at the time of withdrawal. In a Roth IRA, you will be able to withdraw your money tax-free at the time of retirement, but there are certain conditions to it. Please note that there will be some penalty in both the IRAs if you withdraw money before you turn 59 and a half.

- Savings will not happen if you have an attitude of "Save whatever is left after spending." Remember that savings have to be ear-marked at the start of every month. We have discussed this aspect in our earlier sections. Once the money has been assigned to a savings account, you will not be tempted to spend it. It is similar to out of sight, out of mind. You can trick your brain into thinking that you have only a certain amount to help you sustain in any given month.

- The most important step in building a saving corpus is to clear off your debt. Clear off your credit card bills and any other outstanding as that will involve paying interest and late payment fees if you have missed one installment. Continue with adding money to your savings account even in this period so that by the time your debt is cleared, you will have a small corpus ready to handle your emergency requirements.

- In case you make extra income at any given point of time, keep it aside in your savings account. You got your tax-returns, got a bonus at work, a birthday bonus from your employer, or a gift check from your uncle, do not use that money. Add that money in your savings account. As this money was never part of your budget, you will not miss it and will instead inch towards your savings goal.

- Automate your deductions to your savings account. Many people are not able to stick to their budget and end up using their entire account. This behaviour is highly visible in young people, and so the easiest way to save it is to auto-debit your account.

- Question your purchases and think twice before spending your hard-earned money. Be mindful of your expenses. If you have decided to buy something, hold yourself back for a few days and if you still feel that purchase is important, then go ahead and buy it. The other way is to calculate the number of hours you will have to work in order to buy your desired product. Is it worth spending the hours on buying the product? If your answer is yes, then buy it else forget about it.

- You can also try the anti-budget strategy if you are in no mood for keeping track of detailed expenses. In this method, you allot a certain amount to your savings and then you spend the remaining amount as you wish. The entire point of any budget is to keep making headway into savings. So, if you do not intend to keep an item-wise record of your expenditure, match some amount to your savings and spend the remaining amount on utility bills, rent, or groceries. The only thing you need to take care of is to pay your debt first in case you have taken out a loan or used a credit card. You do not want to spend money on interest.

INVESTING

INTRODUCTION TO INVESTING

*H*ave you seen a farmer tirelessly working in the field, removing the weeds, ploughing the field, sowing seeds, watering the field, and patiently waiting to reap the fruits and the harvest? In any investment, a similar approach is required to get the desired benefits. Investment is nothing but a process to buy assets or lend money to get some benefits in the future. The benefits can be in the form of regular payments or increased value of the asset. Investment is an asset that's value will increase over time with compound interest. These assets can be used to fund your various financial goals including retirement, house down-payment, or funding your child's education.

Before we understand the different types of investments and the steps to follow while investing, we should understand what are the different reasons and factors that affect your investment plan ("Introduction to Investing," n.d.).

- Compounding the money or wealth creation is one of the reasons why people invest money. We want our money to grow so that we can meet our financial goals. For this to happen, we have to invest money in different tools depending on our risk taking capacity.
- You want to build a steady source of income that will provide you money as per the rules set by you. Some mutual funds allow you to withdraw money in a planned manner that can supplement your current income. Over a period of time, as your income grows, your dividend and interest also increases, so much that it can become your secondary source of income. Many retirees depend on this interest and dividend as a payment to fund their regular expenses.
- Tax planning is one of the major reasons why people invest. Tax planning is a major exercise in which you look at your earnings both current and projected, and formulate an investment plan that will minimise your taxable income. Moreover, the investment plan should allow to get maximum amount of after-tax returns over the long run, with minimum risk possible.
- The lifecycle of an individual also plays an important role while formulating an investment plan. It has been observed that most of the investors are more aggressive with their investments when they are younger and play more safely as they age. During the

early years, they want to build as much money as possible. They focus on growth-oriented and high-risk investment tools that promise better returns. Mid-age people are more oriented towards consolidating their income. They want high quality investment tools that can promise secure money but at medium risk. They want to fund the family requirements and prefer more bonds than stocks. The later years are focused towards maintaining and maximising your retirement funds. They adopt a highly conservative approach towards investment. They want a steady income source that can fund their retirement and that is why they prefer bonds, certificates of deposits, and other safer options.

- Another important reason to invest is to tackle the monster-inflation. It is one big thing that can eat your money and decrease its value. Inflation is a steady increase in the price of the commodity over time. It decreases the value of the currency. For example, you used to be able to buy a gallon of milk for a few cents, but today, you have to pay a few dollars to get the same quantity. This increase in the cost is called inflation.

- Keeping your money safe in your salary account or savings account will not give you good returns. Ideally, the rate of increase in your income should be greater than inflation rate, so that you can sustain your current lifestyle. The money kept safe in your salary account will reduce in value over time and you will not be able to fund your current lifestyle. Hence, it is advisable to invest, make your money work hard for you, and help you earn returns.

The bottom line is to understand the difference between savings and investments. Yes, it is important to save money, as you need liquid cash for emergency situations like a medical emergency or job loss. It is safe, low-risk, and you will lose less money over time. But investments are equally important. It is advisable to start investing after saving enough money to sustain the expenses for six months. With careful investment planning, you can increase the value of your hard-earned money. If you do not save, you cannot invest, and if you do not invest, the buying capacity of your money reduces.

TYPES OF INVESTMENTS

Organizations are obligated to give a return when you make an investment in their future. They utilize your money in order to grow and give you an expected benefit. The organization can be a government entity or private entity. There are many companies in the market and an investor studies the prospect of the companies and makes the investment based on the judgement. There are many investment options available in the market as every investor tends to think differently. Some believe in playing safe and would invest money in certificate of deposits or a savings account. On the other hand, there are schemes that offer to triple your investment over a period of time. A person decides on the investment depending on the available resources, risk-taking capability, and the future goals of the individual. Based on this, there are many investment options available in the market (Chen, 2019).

A savings account is an investment tool with the lowest risk factor, hence it is the safest and also the easiest way to invest your money. You get a guarantee to get your money back and you know the interest you will earn from your investment. You can remove your money at any point of time and there are no penalty charges.

Certificates of deposits are another tool to save money. We have already read that they are fixed term deposits with terms ranging from 30 days to 10 years. You get your original investment along with the interest earned over the time period and you earn a higher interest than the savings account. The catch here is you will have to pay a penalty in case you want to withdraw your money before the policy matures.

Investments offered by organizations that give a financial claim to the buyer on the issuer's resources are called securities. Bonds, shares, and stocks are some of the types of the securities.

A bond is a fixed income investment tool that is used by the issuer to raise money from the market. The bond issuer takes a loan from the investor and an understanding is signed which includes the details about initial amount and payment terms. Government, public, and private companies use this mode of investment to fund projects. Bonds can have fixed and variable interest rates. They are like a fixed term deposit that gets matured, and the issuer has to give the principal amount along with the agreed interest. A bond is sort of a debt investment where you have lent money to a company and the bond issuer has agreed to pay you interest for a pre-defined time frame and return the principal amount at the end of the time frame (Fernando, 2021).

A mutual fund is a collection of money investments made by more than one investor. This pool of money is then invested in bonds, stocks, and other investment tools. These mutual funds are managed by professional managers and they make investments based on the goals of the investors. The value or performance of your mutual funds portfolio depends on the performance of the individual security your manager decides to buy. Mutual fund investments are different from stock investment as you do not get any voting right. The valuation of the mutual funds happens at the end of the trading day, so the buying and selling of the funds happen after that. They are a type of indirect investment, which means that your investment is a collection of securities that is managed by a professional manager.

Exchange traded funds are funds that are traded throughout the day. This means that their value fluctuates throughout the day. They are easy to trade and have a broader coverage area, which is why they are popular with investors.

Equity or stock is an ongoing investment in a business or a property. This investment makes the investor the owner of the company's assets. The ownership and profit earned is in proportion to the investment made by the investors. A group of stock units is called a share. Stocks are sold and bought on a stock exchange and they form the base of almost every investment portfolio. It is a form of direct investment which means you directly invest your money to get ownership of a portion of the company or business (Hayes, 2021).

There are other investment options like real estate investment in the form of commercial or house mortgages. Commodity investment is another type of investment, which includes oil, gold, silver, agricultural products, and few other commodities.

Investments are also classified as low risk and high risk investments. Risk is defined in terms of ambiguity around the return that the particular investment will generate. A broader range of returns indicate that the risk is higher. The returns on low risk investments are easier to predict, which is why they are deemed as low risk and provide low returns. On the other hand, the returns on high risk investments are difficult to predict but they may provide higher returns. They may also lead to higher loss and that's why the investors should read the terms and conditions properly before investing.

Another way of classifying investment is based on the timeframe. Short term investments are generally for one to three year, and long term investments are for duration more than four years.

With more globalization, investors can also invest in foreign investment tools. Basically, it means investing in firms which are foreign based. These investments may provide greater returns compared to domestic investments.

HOW TO INVEST

In any investment process, there is a supplier and a buyer. The supplier is the one with surplus funds and the buyer is the one who requires the funds. Both the suppliers and buyers come together on a platform to exchange the funds. This marketplace is provided by a financial institution or financial market. Banks and insurance companies are some of the types of financial institutions. Financial markets are platforms where brokers and dealers assist in different types of investments like shares, bonds, commodities, and foreign currency. The equilibrium of price of any investment on both the platforms depends on demand and supply (Gitman et al., 2021/2015).

Investment can be carried out in a series of steps. We will understand these steps and also understand how the factors (impact on personal taxes, life-cycle stage, and external economic environment) affect any investment decision.

1. Ensure that you have sufficient money to fund your basic needs, including your food, utility bills, transportation, housing, and other important needs. Plus, as said earlier, you should have an emergency fund of almost six months worth to fund your daily needs. You should also ensure that you have insurance cover for your medical, life, property, and necessary insurance.
2. Make clear investment goals that define your financial requirements. Some of the common investment goals are:
3. Building retirement funds which will enable you to live comfortably once you retire. The earlier you start planning for your retirement, the higher funds you will accumulate due to the power of compound interest.
4. Saving money to fund some short to long-term goals

like vacations, house downpayment, or funding a business.

5. Investments are also made purely with an intention of wealth creation and accumulation. In this case, the investors believe in the principle of making the money work for you or passive income.

6. Another goal with investments is to save taxes. There are many private and government investment options that allow individuals to save tax by reducing the taxable income.

7. Once you have clearly defined your goals, make an investment plan. It should contain your long term goal, and against that investment goals with investment options written. The options should have an end date and the risk that you are willing to take. The more detailed the plan, the better chances of making an investment plan in lines with your investment goal.

8. In the next step, evaluate the different investment options by taking into consideration the returns, risk factors, and tax benefits. Once the options have been evaluated, carefully select the right set of investment tools.

9. There is an old saying: "Do not put all your eggs in one basket." This saying applies in portfolio management too. Build a diversified investment portfolio as that will reduce your risk factor and also improve your chances to make more profits. You have an option to take professional help by hiring investment managers that carefully design your portfolio to achieve your objectives or you can build a portfolio on your own. The second option is more

    suitable if you have the right set of knowledge or zeal
    to learn.

10. Once the portfolio is created, the real game starts.
    You have to be on top of your finances to understand
    if your investments are making returns as you
    expected. If they are not, you will need to tweak your
    portfolio. One needs to have a dynamic approach
    when it comes to portfolio management.

INVESTMENT STRATEGY AT EVERY AGE

Financial planners usually advise to move away from stocks and move towards bonds as one ages. Young people have more earning age so they can accommodate losses; also, stocks are less risky over a period of time, and young people need a large chunk of money to meet their mid-life requirements like a house down payment, education loans, and other expenses. People who are near their retirement age have more money to invest but less risk-taking capacity as they do not have time to recover from the losses.

We have seen the different investment options in front of an individual. On average, an individual can invest in stocks, bonds, and cash deposits. They also have other investment options like commodities, real estate, and other derivative options. We have learned the importance of maintaining a diversified portfolio. Each investment comes with its own risk and returns level. Depending on the economic condition, an investor makes the investment decision. For example, if the economy is performing well, investors will divert their money into stocks to get higher returns. But if the economy is slow, they will divert their money from stocks to bonds to minimise their losses. The way to manage your portfolio and allot funds is called asset allocation.

When you are in your 20s, you may have recently graduated from college and may be paying off your student loans, so you should start investing in your retirement plans. You can contribute to 401(k) or open an individual retirement account (IRA), and invest whatever small you can afford to invest. You can keep an aggressive attitude towards investment by investing 80% to 90% in stocks and 10% to 20% in bonds. Since you have time in hand, with compound interest you can build a large corpus of money and also can absorb any change in the market.

In your 30s, you should start putting 10% to 15% of your income in investments. You can invest 70% to 80% in stocks and 20% to 30% in bonds. The power of compound interest still applies and you can reap the benefits in the later years. Keep investing in IRA and 401 (K), as this will help you build funds for your retirement. Consider maxing out investment capacity in both IRA and 401(k). Check with your companies if they are contributing to the 401(k). You can also think of investing in real estate as the low interest rate will help to build an asset. Most importantly, invest in yourself in this age group, as skill-building will help to get the much needed promotion or switch to a profile where you can make more money.

Your 40s should be focused more on retirement preparation along with your investment goals like kids' education funding or mortgage payment. Asset allocation may start shifting more towards safer options with 60% allocation in stocks and the remaining in bonds. Remember the more stock options you have in your portfolio, the more volatile and risky your portfolio would be. Understand that you will have to consider inflation while planning for your retirement and therefore make investments in aggressive but safe options (Friedberg, n.d.) .

Your 50s and 60s are the time when you are near your retirement age. You may think of what you have in the accounts and how much funds you will actually require post your retirement. You should consider having a more conservative approach towards your investment. You may allocate your stocks and bonds in the ratio of 50:50. You can think of increasing your investment towards 401(k), as the IRS allows people who are near their retirement age to add more funds to their 401(k). This is called a catch-up contribution and in 2020 and 2021, the IRS allowed an additional $6,500 per year to the existing $19,500 limit to 401(k) funds (Kumok, n.d.).

How you invest will depend on the progress you have made in achieving your financial goals and the economic condition. The key is to start investing early so that you can take advantage of compound interest.

INVESTING FOR BEGINNERS

Whether you are a college graduate starting your first job or in the middle of your career, you should start investing to increase the value of your money. If you do not have the time to learn about investing, you can hire a financial advisor or a mutual funds manager to handle your portfolio, but this will come at a charge. They may charge a percentage of your investment in return for their services. But even then, I would suggest learning the basics of investing so that you can understand better what your advisors are suggesting.

Before we get into learning how to invest for first-timers, let us look at some typical personality types you will observe in the investment world.

The "Doomsday Preppers" are people who believe that the financial world will not last and that is why they invest mostly in gold and real estate. The "Gambling-Day Traders" are serious gamblers but instead of gambling in a casino, they gamble in the stock market. They closely monitor the stock market like a hawk every second the day and buy and sell stocks on an hourly basis. The "Indexers" invest in all the available options and watch their income in a slow and steady manner (Town, 2018).

As the first step, you decide whether you need professional help or not. As I have mentioned, you can hire a professional portfolio manager if you don't have the time to learn the nuances of investing. Another option that is quite popular nowadays is robo-advisors. They are virtual financial advisors that offer you the best advice based on an algorithm created by the financial institution. They are easy to use, affordable, and more convenient to use. You do not have to pay any brokerage fees associated with using their services. Here are some options for robo-advisors:

No initial investment is required to open an account with Betterment. An annual fee of 0.25% each year is levied for the management of the account. The app allows you to choose from thousands of stocks and ETFs available in the US and internationally. Based on your preference and risk taking capacity, you can build a customized portfolio and plus you will have your account managed.

With Wealthfront, you will require only $500 to start your investment journey. There are no fees until your investment touches $10,000, and post that, a minimal amount of 0.25% per year will be charged. Once your budget goals are met, your money can be automatically transferred to an investment account with a Wealthfront Cash Account.

M1 Finance offers both robo-advisor and traditional brokerage under the same umbrella. You can start investing with as little as $100 with this user-friendly app. There are no fees at all for either opening an account or trading.

You can have your portfolio managed by Vanguard Digital Advisor® once you have $3,000 to invest. They will build a customized portfolio based on your goals and risk-taking ability. The portfolio will include ETFs, which are generally at low cost. The target annual net advisory fee is about 0.15% of your Digital Advisor balance. They also offer a dashboard and built-in tools that will help you streamline your investment process and also be able to check how even a small amount will impact your retirement savings.

Once you have decided which help to take, you need to decide how much money to invest. Before you start investing, you need to keep your emergency funds aside. Follow the rule of 50-30-20, and invest the recommended amount. Start early so that you can take advantage of the compound interest and build the maximum wealth possible. Your investment amount will also depend on your financial goals.

Now that you know the amount that you will be investing every month, we will look into the investment options available. In the initial duration, follow a simple investment strategy. When deciding on your investment portfolio, consider the below two factors:

- Allocate your funds properly and create a well-chosen mix of bonds, stocks, commodity, and cash investments.
- Create an automated investment plan so that you would not make decisions based on your emotions.
- Have patience and allow your portfolio to grow.

We already have discussed the various investment options available in the market. The key is to research and learn about the investment tool and the companies you will be investing in. Investment in the stock market has the potential to give the maximum returns, but you have to be careful in your research and invest accordingly. You cannot invest randomly and expect a huge return on that; instead you will end up losing money. Do not get swayed by ads or your friend's advice. Do your homework on the company and then invest your hard-earned money.

HOW TO START INVESTING IN STOCKS

In most of the cases, investing in stocks equates to buying shares in any company. By investing in the company's stock, you hope that the company will perform well and will earn money. If the company grows, then the value of the shares increases, and you will be able to sell at a price higher than what you paid for them. So, basically when you sell the stocks, you will earn profit. With increased usage of technology in finance or in short fintech, investing in stocks has become more accessible and easier. Anyone with minimum knowledge can open an account via a website or an app and start investing. You can earn profit from stocks in two ways: dividend payments and selling shares at a higher price than you paid for them to purchase.

Mode of Investing

You will have to first open a brokerage account, which is an account that you can sell and buy stocks, bonds, and mutual funds. You can open the account online and in most of the cases, there is no requirement of initial deposit. You will have to transfer funds to your account before you are allowed to buy or sell stocks. If you want to manage your accounts on your own, you can open an online brokerage account. You can buy or sell stocks using the broker's website. In case you want someone to manage your account, you can hire a professional or use the services of a robo-advisor. At the time of opening the account, you may be asked if you want to open a cash account or margin account. Cash account is opened with your cash, whereas in a margin account, you borrow money from the broker to purchase stocks in exchange for some interest charges. It is advised to stick to a cash account as a margin account is risky (O'Shea, 2021).

The amount that you transfer to a cash account depends on your economic condition, investment goals, and risk taking capacity. Also, note that stock investments are generally advised for long-term investments so as to minimize the risk factor.

Have an Investment Strategy

If you have hired an expert to manage your account or if you have taken the services of a robo-advisor, you will not have to worry about your portfolio. Generally, they ask you about your investment goals, the amount you have, and then build a customized portfolio for you. In case of a human advisor, they may charge a certain percentage of your investments. A robo-advisor firm usually charges 0.25% of your investment.

In case you have decided to follow a DIY approach, then you should build a proper investment strategy. Normally for any beginner, there are two types of investments:

- Index funds are typically made up of bonds and stocks, and they track the market index. A stock market usually collects data from different companies on the index and presents a picture of how they are performing. There are many indexes and the S&P 500 Index is the most popular index. S&P 500 index stands for Stand and Poor's 500 index, has 500 of the largest companies in the US, and is generally considered to tell how well the US stocks are performing (Caplinger, n.d.). The other popular indexes based on their market cap are (Caplinger, n.d.-a):
- Large U.S. stocks: S&P 500, Dow Jones Industrial Average, Nasdaq Composite
- Small U.S. stocks: Russell 2000, S&P SmallCap 600
- International stocks: MSCI EAFE, MSCI Emerging Markets
- Bonds: Bloomberg Barclays Global Aggregate Bond
- Individual stocks can be purchased if you have the

patience and time to research about every single
stock that you are planning to buy.

You should always diversify your portfolio so that you can reduce your risk. Invest in businesses the basics of which you can understand, play safe, and avoid highly volatile investments until you are confident in your skills. Avoid buying stocks that cost you less than $5, also called penny stocks. They have a notorious reputation as many investors have lost money in these stocks. Most importantly, learn how to research and evaluate companies before you invest.

How to Choose Stocks and Shares to Invest In

When it comes to choosing stock and shares to invest in, you may consider the below factors (Hyett, n.d.):

- External economic condition
- Look into the future
- Buy brands you love and know

External economic condition: Every economy in this world goes through the cycle of growth and then decline. When the economy is booming, there is more money in the market and people spend more money. But when the economy starts declining, the spending reduces. You may want to follow this cycle and buy stocks and shares accordingly.

Looking at this, we have many defensive shares or cyclical shares. Defensive shares are usually steady in their growth. They may not grow massively during boom but they are also not reduced drastically during tough times. This is because most of the companies that fall under this group, have products or services that people may use irrespective of the economic cycle. Pharmaceuticals and FMCG companies are some of the examples of these shares. This is because people will eat and require medicines irrespective of the economic cycle.

Cyclical shares as the names suggest depend on the economic condition. They perform well during boom and surfer during slow times. Usually people buy shares during slump and sell off during peak times. These shares are not affected at the same time. For example, retailers will be first one to get affected during a slump, followed by distributors and then manufacturers.

Major cyclical sectors: aerospace, automotive, banks, construction, engineering and industrials, media, manufacturing, mining, property, retailing, and travel and leisure.

Major defensive sectors: food, beverages, healthcare, household goods, life insurance, pharmaceuticals, support services , tobacco, and water.

Look into the future: People who anticipated the boom in information and technology, and invested in technology companies, earned millions in dividends and profits. In developing nations, the buying capacity of the middle class is increasing, which has led to an increase in demand for luxury products like better cars, smartphones, and other luxurious products. This approach is not always successful as at times companies fail to innovate and are replaced by better products. For example, Xerox faded out and was replaced by other technology giants. With the pandemic, the stock options of IT companies and pharma companies have skyrocketed, though this is more of a once in a lifetime event which could not have been predicted by anyone.

But sectors like technology, pharmaceuticals, and also renewable sources of energy like electric cars, are to be watched out for. With increasing oil prices and climate change affecting the world, many companies are looking for replacements. Tesla was an innovator in this segment, and people who invested in this have earned a lot.

Look for brands that sell: Have you noticed that the world's biggest brands are also the most profitable? With the amazing products and after sales services, some products managed to create a high brand equity. This also reflects in their stock performance. The most obvious benefit of investing in a famous brand is that, since you have already used it, you are aware of the plus points and you know that the sales will increase and the company will perform well. The only negative point is that the selling price of these shares is usually high and you can buy less number of shares depending on your buying capacity.

Watch Your Stocks and Continue Investing

Whatever mode you adopt, you should be prepared to be in this game for a long haul to get the desired returns. Stock markets are known to have volatile behaviour, and you should be capable enough to continue to be invested even during economic turmoil. Unless you are a compulsive day trader, you should avoid looking at your stock on a daily basis. I would advise you to buy the stock and then check on them only a few times a year to ensure that the growth is in-line with your investment goals. Do not follow too much news and keep your long-term goal in perspective.

INSURANCE AND COVER

INSURANCE AND TYPES OF INSURANCE

*I*nsurance is a type of financial protection that is offered to a party against some fees paid by said party. It is basically a kind of risk mitigation tool which is used to hedge the risk against a potential loss. Usually in any insurance policy, there are two parties involved: insurer and insured. The insurance provider is called an insurer (i.e. the insurance company) and the person who buys insurance is called an insured.

When the insurer and insured enter a contract, it is called insurance policy, which has the details about the amount the insured has to pay and the conditions under which the insured will be compensated financially by the insurer. The amount paid by the insured is called a premium. In case of any eventuality, the insured submits a claim to the insurance company, which is then investigated and verified by the claims adjuster. Before the insured gets the claim, the person has to pay a deductible (also called a co-payment in health insurance), which is an out of pocket payment. The insurer earns money by putting the insured money in the stock market, or it can mitigate the risk by re-insuring the amount. So, in short, any insurance policy generally will have the following elements: clear names of the insurer, insured, and the beneficiaries, the premium amount, duration of the coverage, detail about the events under which the loss would be covered, amount that will be paid to the policyholder or the beneficiary, and any events which will not be covered or protected by the policy. This policy then indemnifies the insured party against the damage. The insurers get premiums from multiple parties, and as long as the insurer has kept funds aside for claims (also called reserves), the remaining money is the insurer's profit ("Insurance," 2021).

Characteristics of Insurance Policies

For any item or person to be insured as a risk, it should meet certain characteristics.

The insurance company will first check the insurability of the risk or the capability of the risk to be deemed worth insuring. Some of the factors are ("Insurance," 2021):

1. Large number of exposure units: Insurance is based on the law of large numbers. For any risk to be insurable, there should be a large number of exposure units of the similar kind so that the losses can be predicted. The insurance company, when they have compiled the loss data in large, it is easier for

them to predict the amount of loss more accurately and hence can determine the premium accordingly.

2. Ability of the loss to be defined and measured: The other characteristic is that risk should be defined and measurable. One should be able to provide proof of loss in absolute numbers so that a premium can be defined properly. The policyholder should provide bills which can define the value of the risk. If the value of the loss or damage cannot be defined, it cannot be insured. Life and death of any person can be fairly determined and hence payment paid against the claim is the value of the amount insured.

3. Probability should be predictable: The insurers should be able to define the probability of the risk happening. They must be able to define how often the loss will occur and the severity of the loss. Certain losses cannot be protected, as it is difficult to determine the probability of them occurring.

4. Chance events should be calculable: The insurance company should be able to determine the chance of risk to happen. The risk should be a chance and accidental event, where the exact timing and impact of the loss cannot be defined.

5. Size of the loss: The loss should be large enough so that it will make sense for the insured to pay the premium. The costs include administration charges, money adjusted against, and others. All these costs will not make any sense if the protection offered does not offer any value to the policy holder.

6. The risk should be non-catastrophic: There are two types of catastrophic risks- first type of risk when the policyholders are exposed to the same kind of

event, like in case of floods or earthquakes. In the second type of risk, the insurers are unable to determine the probability of the risk happening or the loss that will be incurred from the event like in case of a terrorist attack.

7. The premium cost should be affordable: The premium should be economically feasible for both the parties. The insured should be able to afford the premium and the insurer should be able to make some profits.

Legal Aspects of Insurance Policy

In any insurance policy, there are legal requirements and regulations. Some of the common points raised are ("Insurance," 2021):

- The insured is compensated or indemnified by the insurance company in case of certain loss upto the insured's interest.
- Under benefit interest the insurance company cannot recover from the party who caused the damage or injury. They should compensate the insured party irrespective of whether the policyholder has sued the damage causing party or not.
- Under insurable interest the policyholder should have directly suffered from the damage or loss in the form of property damage or human loss. They should have a stake in the damage so that they can raise a claim for the same. This refers to the interest of the policyholder in obtaining the

insurance. In short, if the policyholder will suffer a loss if the insured property or person is damaged or injured.

- The policyholder and the insurer share a bond of faith and honesty under uberrima fides. All the material facts of both the parties should be declared.
- In the principle of contribution which comes from indemnity, if multiple insurance providers are involved, all of them will make a contribution to the claim made by the policyholder.
- In subrogation, the insured transfers the legal rights to the insurance company to recover the damage incurred by a third party. The insurance company may sue the third party or take any other legal action deemed appropriate.
- In causa proxima, or proximate cause, the main cause behind the damage is identified. If the main cause is covered in the insurance policy, the insurance company has to pay for the damages as per the conditions mentioned in the policy.
- Under mitigation, the insured should always try to minimize the loss due to damage to a property or human loss. They should behave as if the asset is not insured.
- Indemnification is an important principle of insurance policy. The literal meaning of indemnification is to reinstate a property to its original position as much as possible the way it was before the damage was incurred. Life insurance is not generally an indemnity insurance; instead, it is considered a contingent insurance. This means that a claim will be raised if the damage has occurred due

to any particular event. The insured can be indemnified under three contracts

- A "reimbursement" policy
- A "pay on behalf" or "on behalf of policy"
- An "indemnification" policy

In all the above contracts, the insured will be paid by the insurance company. Under reimbursement policy, the insured has to pay for the repair or replacement out of the pocket and can later claim for the reimbursement. The insured should carry out the repair or replacement with permission from the insurer for the claim to be accepted and fulfilled.

In pay on behalf policy, the insured would not pay anything out of the pocket. The insurance company would negotiate on behalf of the insured and pay any claim raised. Lately, most insurance policies use this type of contract, as it makes it easier for the insurance company to manage the claim and control the expenses.

When it comes to indemnification policy, the insurance company can use any of the above-mentioned contract types that are a reimbursement or pay on behalf. The usage depends on which contract is more beneficial to the insured and insurer during the claim handling process.

The policy usually does not include causes like a nuclear exclusion clause, excluding damage caused by nuclear and radiation accidents, and a war exclusion clause, excluding damage from acts of war or terrorism.

PROPERTY INSURANCE

Property insurance is a type of policy that provides protection for the property or provides liability coverage. When the property of a third party is damaged unintentionally by the insured, the damage to property or individuals can be covered by the property insurance when the claim is raised and if they are found to be legal. Home insurance, flood insurance, renters insurance, and earthquake insurance are some of the types of property insurance.

Property insurance provides three types of coverage:

- The cost involved in repairing or replacing the damaged property at the same value is called replacement cost. One gets the replacement cost rather than the actual value of the damaged item.
- In actual cash value coverage, the owner gets the actual cost of the item minus the depreciation. For example, if the cost of a damaged item was $100 five years ago, and the cost today is $150, you will get$100.
- In extended replacement cost coverage, the individual will get up to 25% more money than the coverage limit, in case the cost of construction has increased.

Home Insurance

As mentioned earlier, home insurance is a type of property insurance that provides financial protection against damage or theft to a residence along with damage to assets or contents of the house. Each home insurance policy has a liability limit that defines the coverage offered to the insured. A home insurance offers protection against four types of damage: damage done to the interiors of the home, any external damage to the home, loss or damage of personal assets/belongings, and injury that occurs while on the property. The homemaker will have to pay a deductible while making a claim against any of the above mentioned damage.

The standard liability limits are usually $100,000, but the insured has the option to go for a higher limit. If a claim is made, the liability limit determines the amount that will go towards repairing or replacing the damage to building, personal imtema, and also the cost of living in a separate property while the repairs are being made.

Earthquakes, floods or any act of God or damage done due to a war, or damage done due to mold, are generally not covered by standard home insurance policies. Homeowners living in areas prone to earthquakes or any natural disasters can apply for special coverage to protect against damage done by these acts. But most basic homeowners insurance policies cover events like hurricanes and tornadoes.

The claims made against mentioned perils in the contract are accepted by the insurance companies. An official from the insurance company may come to your house to investigate and confirm if the property was damaged by a mentioned peril. There is another section in the home insurance, which is called open peril, which provides against all the perils except those excluded from the contract.

Under home insurance, the contents of the home are also insured. Most insurance policies provide coverage for personal contents during a move to a new place or when you are on a vacation. It is advisable to check with your insurance provider on the coverage provided by them and ensure **accidental damage is covered**. In some cases, one may opt for additional coverage for personal possessions to provide protection while moving to a different place. This extra is policy or rider provides protection for two types of items:

Personal possessions are items that you normally carry with you while moving from your place. You will be asked about the coverage that you need when you choose this option. Choose a sum total of the amount of the value of the items that you carry.

Specified items are any high risk item that costs more than a specified amount. Some of the high risk items are computers, laptops, tablets, notebooks, jewellery, watches, pearls, precious metals or stones, and other items. Some of the high-end policies have higher limits, less number of exclusions, and at times better settlement conditions.

MORTGAGE INSURANCE AND HOW IT WORKS

Mortgage insurance is a policy that offers protection to the lenders and compensates them in case of the default of the mortgage loan, when the borrower passes away or is unable to pay the amount due to any circumstance. This insurance is usually of three types: private mortgage insurance, qualified mortgage insurance premium, and mortgage title insurance (Kagan, 2020).

- Private mortgage insurance, or PMI, is required if the borrower is unable to pay the mandatory 20% down payment while buying a property. The PMI is arranged by the lender and provided by private insurance firms. Use the PMI calculator to understand the amount of premium you will have to pay. Usually it is part of your monthly installments and it can be canceled once your down payment of 20% has been covered.

- Qualified mortgage insurance premium is paid to provide protection against borrower's mortgage payments. Most loans approved by the US Federal Housing Administration also include the mortgage insurance premium and an annual premium, regardless of the down payment amount. The premium amount is 1.75% of the loan amount, and the annual premium ranges from 0.45% to 1.05% of the average outstanding balance of the loan for that year. If the down payment is less than 10%, then one has to pay the monthly installments of the premium for the entire duration of the FHA loan, and if the downpayment is over 10%, then the premium has to be paid for 11 years (Marquand & Bundrick, 2021).
- Mortgage title insurance protects the lenders and the borrowers from any damages caused by a bad title. A thorough search of the title is conducted by the lawyer or the title company professional to check if the property has not been leased, or if the current owner is the rightful owner of the property. Even after the search, it may happen that the title may go bad. This is where title insurance protects the buyer and the lender.

How Does Mortgage Insurance Work?

In this type of insurance, the borrower pays the premium but the benefit is availed by the lender. The insurance can be paid as a fixed amount entirely at the time of signing the mortgage or on a monthly basis. The lender will get a portion from the premium amount that the borrower pays in case the borrower stops paying the installment.

Also, note that the mortgage insurance is different from the mortgage protection insurance as in this insurance the lender gets paid in case the borrower dies. However, the borrower gets no benefit and it is advised to get term life insurance. In case the borrower dies, the lender will get the mortgage paid and your house will become mortgage free but your family will have no say in how the amount can be utilized. This insurance locks your money, and forces your family to pay the mortgage even if there are more urgent needs in front of your family.

LIFE INSURANCE AND HOW TO CHOOSE THE BEST OPTION

Life insurance is a policy in which you pay premiums in exchange of a guarantee that your family or the beneficiary you have assigned will get the insured amount in the event of your death. You need life insurance so that your business and family can continue to function even after your death. The most common life insurance policies are term life insurance and whole life insurance. Life insurance covers death caused by natural causes, car accidents, or any death that is not excluded at the time of signing the policy.

Life insurance would not cover death caused by suicide, murder by the beneficiary, or murder caused during willing criminal activity. It may also not cover death caused by death-defying stunts or any dangerous act, or if you have lied at the time of signing the policy. For example, if you lied about your underlying health condition, the life insurance will not pay anything. Some of the factors that affect your premium amount are height, weight, age, gender, present and past health condition, family health history, smoking and drinking habits, occupation, lifestyle, and other factors.

Term life insurance is offered for a particular time period like 10, 20, or 30 years. During the time period you will pay the premiums and in case you die during the period, your beneficiary will get the insured amount. In case of no death, no amount is paid.

In whole life insurance, your policy remains active as long as you continue to pay the premiums. The insurance company is liable to pay the insured amount in the eventuality of your death and if your policy is still active. Whole life policy costs more premium payment compared to term life insurance.

What to Consider When Buying Life Insurance?

- The cost of the premium is one of the important factors to consider before buying the policy. Many factors affect the cost of the premium in which age is the most important factor. The younger you buy the policy, the less you will have to pay for the premium, although your premium increases if you smoke, drink, or have any underlying health condition. Reach out to multiple vendors, negotiate, and get the best deal for your life insurance policy.
- The term length comes into picture in case you are

signing a term life insurance policy. As I have mentioned earlier, the term period ranges from 10 to 30 years. As the chances of your death increases as you age, in case of longer duration term policy, the rates of the policy premiums will also increase. Hence, the policy premium rate for 30 years will be higher than one for 10 years.

- Check for flexibility in the policy. In many cases, if you have purchased, you are stuck with the terms and conditions of the policy for the entire duration. But in some cases, especially online, companies allow more flexibility, especially changing the duration of the term either reducing or increasing the duration. They also allow you to cancel the policy.

- As this policy is related to the death of the individual, the life insurance companies require some details to check your qualification for the policy. They stress on details related to your health and lifestyle. They may ask you to go through a medical examination and get the medical reports so as to ascertain your current health situation and charge your premium accordingly. But nowadays, new insurtech companies are utilising data related to your health, spending habits, and lifestyle details to determine your chances of getting the insurance. They may allow you to skip medical examinations altogether.

- Success ratio of the life insurance companies should also be considered before buying the policy. You should check the ease factor with which they give the payout, the success ratio in terms of the companies processing time taken to settle the claim and send the money to the beneficiary without much hassle.

- One should also consider the time taken for the policy to go live and be delivered to you. The traditional firms take around three to eight weeks to send you the policy. But many insurtech companies have reduced the processing time and deliver the policy in your inbox within a few days.
- You should consider the payout method for your life insurance policy. The payout can be in the form of a lump sum amount or monthly payments. In case of lump sum amount, the payout happens in one amount which can be utilised by the beneficiaries. With monthly payments, the beneficiary will get a monthly payment, which can be to pay off monthly bills, but once the policy term ends, the payment will stop. For example, if you die a few months before the policy lapses, the payout will happen only for the remaining few months and post that, no money will be given.

When to Consider and When Not to Consider Buying Life Insurance?

Buying life insurance is helpful to fund your family needs even when you are gone. We will look into situations when one should consider buying a life insurance policy.

- People with dependents should consider buying a life insurance policy. If you are a parent, it is advisable to buy life insurance unless you have a considerable amount of savings or good retirement funds. We all have heard stories about families having to downgrade their lifestyle because the earning member or one of the earning members of their family died without leaving much savings. With education becoming expensive and inflation eating away the salary, it may be difficult on a single person's salary. If you buy life insurance, your loved ones would not have to suffer once you are not there. It is important that both parents should buy a life insurance policy, even if one person is staying at home, as the additional money will help to fund the needs of the dependents.

- People with partners or having joint home mortgages should consider buying term life insurance. In case of death of any one of the partners, the other would find it easier to pay off the mortgage. Remember, life insurance not only provides money to fund the needs of the family, it also reduces the stress of the family and provides protection to the family when the tragedy strikes.

- It is at times advised by some experts that people without any dependents should not consider buying a life insurance policy. It may work if you have created a trust fund that has sufficient money to take care of your funeral arrangements and also pay off your financial liabilities, if any, post your death. But if you do not want to create a trust fund, you may consider buying a whole life insurance policy that will take care of all the expenses and debts post your death. Additionally, you should create a will that clearly clarifies what should be done with any life insurance money.

If you are considering buying a policy, you should research and consider all the factors before deciding to buy the policy. In case you have dependents, you should consider buying a policy so that your loved ones can continue with the same lifestyle.

RETIREMENT PLANNING

⚜

*U*ntil now, we have learned about the various aspects of personal finance, including budgeting, investments, savings, and insurance. We will now look into the final aspect of a sound financial plan, which is retirement planning.

INTRODUCTION TO RETIREMENT PLANNING AND IMPORTANCE

Retirement planning is a life-long process that involves defining your retirement goals, and chalking out the steps and decisions that will enable the fulfilment of these goals. Essentially, retirement planning involves determining the age you want to retire, identifying the different sources of income and the expenses based on needs, wants and emergency funds, chalking out the different investment options available, and determining the best ones that will help to achieve the retirement goals. Retirement planning is about creating a plan that will prepare you to live a life when the regular income stops coming. It involves planning not just the financial aspect of life, but also factors like how you will spend your time, your living conditions, if you would have to continue working part time to fund your lifestyle, and other important aspects. Retirement planning changes according to the different stages of life. In the initial part of your career, you will save a lump sum amount towards your mid-career, and you will realise the actual amount you will need to retire. You will then divert your funds accordingly and take steps to achieve the desired amount. And once you have retired, it will be about distributing the accumulated fund over the years so that you can live comfortably post retirement (Kagan, 2019).

Since the early 2000s, retirement planning has moved from an employer-based to individual-based model. With this transition, it has become highly important for people to save, invest, and be fully equipped to fund their retirement goals. Unfortunately, not many people understand the concept of compound interest, inflation, diversification of portfolio to reduce the risk factor. Owing to that, they fail to plan their retirement properly, even when their retirement is due in a few years. This negligence in retirement planning results in having low retirement funds and facing problems once the regular income has stopped crediting to the account.

According to a study (Mitchell & Lusardi, 2011) , financial literacy was lowest in the age group of people younger than 35 years or older than 65 years. This fact indicates that these groups are not equipped with the right knowledge to increase their retirement fund. They lack financial knowledge and hence fail to plan for their retirement. This gap is worrisome as being able to formulate and implement a retirement plan is the key to retirement security. It was observed that those who did not have a proper retirement plan retired with half the amount compared to the people who had planned their retirement. It may be because the financially illiterate people lack the knowledge of compound interest both in terms of investment and credit card usage. As we have seen when we use a credit card, the interest levied is compounding in nature, which means that we end up paying a significant amount to the creditor and reduce our savings. Also, if we do not start investing early, we may lose out on significant interest earnings based on the power of compounding. Unfortunately, this indicates that the people who are less educated and have low wages may have bad financial decision making ability. This inability will impact their personal finance, and in turn, their decisions related to investments, spending, and most importantly retirement.

A council on financial literacy started by former President Barack Obama stated, "While the crisis has many causes, it is undeniable that financial illiteracy is one of the root causes... Sadly, far too many Americans do not have the basic financial skills necessary to develop and maintain a budget, to understand credit, to understand investment vehicles, or to take advantage of our banking system. It is essential to provide basic financial education that allows people to better navigate an economic crisis such as this one" (Department, n.d.). This statement indicates that financial literacy is not widespread in the country and also how being financially literate can help you to understand your investments better and ultimately plan your retirement in a better way (Mitchell & Lusardi, 2011).

Retirement planning not only provides you financial relief, it is also important for your mental health. It has been observed that people who have planned their retirement feel less stressed and depressed. If you participate in early retirement planning, you will have more positive experience in adjusting to your life post retirement. Also, a study has shared that if you have planned your retirement well, you can more easily and early opt out of the working life. American Psychiatric Association has estimated that over 70% of people are stressed about their financial health and that can also affect your physical health.

If you have planned your retirement funds properly, you will not have to pay a lot of taxes in your retirement. Also, retirement planning has a lot of tax benefits during your working tenure. Plans like 401(k), traditional IRA, and Roth IRA can help to reduce your taxes during working tenure. From a tax-benefit point of view, you will have following income sources during your retirement:

- Tax-deferred investment includes pension plans, social security, 401 (k)s, and pre-tax IRAs.
- Tax-free investment includes Roth IRAs, Health Savings Accounts (HSAs), and municipal bonds.
- Tax-managed investment includes standard brokerage accounts with tax-efficient investments like index funds.

Also, when you have a bigger amount and retirement lifestyle in mind, you will plan your career moves accordingly and aim to increase your income to fund that lifestyle. In case you are forced to take an early retirement, you would not be caught off guard and be better prepared to handle the tough situation. Most importantly, you will be able to continue to lead an independent life where your self-respect will be left intact. You would not have to depend on your children or anyone to fund your daily needs. When you have planned for your medical emergencies, including long-term, you would not have to rely on external help.

RETIREMENT PLANNING AND RETIREMENT SATISFACTION

We have seen the importance of retirement planning in the earlier sections. A good retirement plan will make you feel secure and independent in your old age. Like it is important to look after your physical health right from a young age, similarly it is important to secure your retirement right from your first job. With an increase in the lifespan of an individual, we live longer, and hence it is important to plan your financial health properly so that you can live an independent and a secure life.

Generally, people who have been planning for their retirement well in advance are more satisfied and happy in their life post-retirement. According to a study (Elder, 1999), in most cases, a substantial drop in household consumption is observed post-retirement. It may be because the people who manage to save less have to reduce their consumption compared to people who have planned their retirement well. If one has to make some lifestyle changes, it reduces the satisfaction level. The other reason may be that the actual retirement fund required is not gauged properly by the individual and hence they are caught off-guard. These people have been observed to be less satisfied in their lives compared to people who have planned their retirement well due to stark difference in the perceived and actual requirement of retirement funds. The study also highlighted that over 65% of people who attended the retirement planning meetings were very satisfied compared to 36.7% of people who did not attend any retirement planning meeting. Apart from economic factors like accumulated wealth, non-economic factors like health condition, marital status, and the reasons also affect the retirement satisfaction. It was also observed that people who were forced to retire due to poor health or who were let go by the employer for other reasons were found to be less satisfied as they did not get proper time to plan for their retirement.

Some researchers have suggested that with the passage of time, your satisfaction with retirement also changes. In the initial days of retirement, the satisfaction is lower compared to the later days, when a routine has been formed. This can be rectified by proper retirement planning, as that allows retirees to form some realistic retirement goals from a financial, mental, and physical well-being standpoint. With realistic expectations of retirement life, an employee can plan their retirement age properly as well as leave the organization feeling more satisfied. With clear retirement planning, one can set realistic financial goals and take necessary actions to achieve those financial goals. When the goals are achieved, it will lead to a more satisfied retired life. Planning your retired life will positively impact both concrete factors like physical and financial health and abstract factors like social life, and lead to a more satisfied post-retirement life. The research also suggests that people in high paying jobs are more likely to take up financial planning for their retirement compared to people who are in lower income groups and low skilled jobs (PhD & PhD, 2021/2003).

So, retirement planning plays a significant role if you want to lead a highly satisfied post retirement life. Planning will help to be prepared for the unexpected and avoid any unpleasant surprises that may affect your retirement corpus fund.

HOW MUCH DO YOU NEED FOR RETIREMENT PLANNING

In your younger days, if you have a debt-free life, keep your credit bills at the minimum, and have disposable income, you should invest for your short-term and long-term goals. Amongst your various short-term goals, building a corpus nest of six months to fund your daily needs should be your top most priority. For long-term planning, it is your retirement that you should plan for. Retirement is the time when your regular monthly salary will stop being credited to your account. So, it is important to have a plan where enough money is credited to your account so that you can continue with the same lifestyle. Looking at inflation and rising medical costs, here is the important question that you should ask yourself before you start planning: *How much money do I need for a comfortable living post-retirement?*

Is Investing Money Better Than Savings?

According to research (Probasco, 2020) (2019 401(k) Participant Survey, 2019), on average, retirees need $1.7 million to retire comfortably, and very few are on the way to achieving that target. Most of the time, this is because people are not aware how much to save, they do not know what investment tools to use, and they do not track how much has been saved. The research indicates that 95% of people would like professional help to determine their retirement goals. Apart from determining the age to retire, for which 41% of the people seek professional help, 40% of the people would like to know about the amount that they should save before their retirement. The research also indicates that 38% of the people are stressed about their retirement plans and saving enough money to retire comfortably.

The same research says that 64% of people were more into saving than investing. This high percentage indicates that most people end up putting money into savings accounts instead of using options like an individual retirement account, health savings account, or real estate. This approach will not help in the long run, as the interest you earn on your savings account is significantly lower than the interest you will earn by investing in the stock market or IRA. Almost 50% of the people have not made any changes to the investment portfolio of 401(k) in two years. Following a "set up and forget" approach will be detrimental in the long run, when you will realise that your money has not grown the way it should have. It is important to be actively involved in managing your 401(k) plans to make it grow and the approach applies to your retirement investment tools too.

Some Approaches to Determine How Much Would You Need

Write down your retirement goals and then add cost against each line item. Factor in the inflation rate. On average, the inflation rate in the US has been around 2% for the last few years and even the federal government benchmarks the inflation rate at 2% (Lake, n.d.-a). Keeping this inflation rate in mind, plan your retirement expenses. You should factor in the rising medical costs, in case you do not have health insurance. On the other side, make a list of your possible sources of income. Apart from your 401 (k), it may include house rents, social security, pension, and other sources that you can create. Add up your expenses and your income, and aim to match them. The amount that you get on your expenses side can be the starting point for your retirement planning. Some of the expenses that you may include in your column are utility bills, house maintenance costs, grocery, travel expenditures, and life insurance. Healthcare will be a major area where you will have to contribute significantly. According to an estimate, a 65 year old person living in the US in 2020 will require $295,000 in healthcare during their retirement years (Lake, n.d.-a).

There are experts that suggest the retirement income should be approximately 80% of your final pre-retirement salary. The amount may differ depending on your post retirement choices or if you plan to work part-time post retirement.

Another popular way to determine the amount is the 4% rule. This rule is applied to determine the amount that a retired person can withdraw from their retirement savings account to maintain a steady source of income. Here, your income depends on the dividends and interest you earn on the corpus fund. Suppose you require $100,000 post your retirement annually to sustain your lifestyle. So, according to the 4% rule, you would require $2,500,000 at the time of your retirement. But experts today consider this rule outdated as it does not consider the dynamic market conditions. Also, the success of this rule will depend on how strictly you follow the approach. In case you spurge one year, your entire planning will go for a toss, as your interest and dividends will reduce.

Now you will look into formulas to determine your saving goals based on your current income level.

Percentage of Your Salary

One of the ways to determine the amount one should accumulate at various age groups can be to think in terms of the percentage of your salary (Probasco, 2020). It is suggested that your savings should be equal to your salary by the time you become 30. This figure can be approached by saving 15% of your gross salary starting from when you were 25 and out of this 15%, half this amount should be invested in stocks. The percentages for other other age groups are

- Age 40—two times annual salary
- Age 50—four times annual salary
- Age 60—six times annual salary
- Age 67—eight times annual salary

Another way to achieve the savings equal to your salary when you become 30, is to be more aggressive. You should aim to save 25% of your annual salary starting in your 20s. This 25% may include your 401 (k), employer contribution, stock investments, and various other types of investment options that we have discussed. If we continue with the savings logic, then here are the benchmarks for other age groups.

- Age 35—two times annual salary
- Age 40—three times annual salary
- Age 45—four times annual salary
- Age 50—five times annual salary
- Age 55—six times annual salary
- Age 60—seven times annual salary
- Age 65—eight times annual salary

STEPS FOR RETIREMENT PLANNING

Retirement planning is crucial for you to be able to continue with the same lifestyle and also look after your medical needs. Generally, there are five steps that you should follow for good retirement planning (Orem, 2021):

- Knowing when you want to retire depends on when you have accumulated enough to replace your regular monthly income. For that we have to understand the different sources of income that will fund your retirement. The most common source is social security. The average amount that you can receive monthly in 2021 is $1,543. The full retirement age is 66 years, but in the case of people born after 1960, the full retirement age has been increased to 67 years. At the full retirement age, you can get $3,148 monthly and if you apply for social security when you reach 70 years, you can get $3,895 monthly. Also, check if you have a pension provided by your employer. You can also fund your retirement by taking up an additional job or doing a part time job post retirement. Once you have income sources listed, add your expenses, which should clearly define your needs, wants, and emergency funds (Weston, 2021).

- Once you know when you want to retire, the next step would be to know how much money you will require at the time of your retirement. Jot down your future expenses, including medical expenses, and then match your future income to your expenses. This can be your starting point. We have spoken about the steps involved in determining the amount and the plan you should follow to reach that desired amount.

- Phase out your financial goals in terms of their importance. Apart from retirement planning, you must have other financial goals that may be more important at any given point of time. It may be your child's education fees or home mortgage down payment. Most importantly, you have to plan your emergency fund before you start planning for any other financial goal. So, create a priority list and fund your goals accordingly. Ideally speaking, you should continue to fund your retirement goals along with your other financial goals.

- Now that you know how much to save, it is important to know how to invest and achieve that amount. We will now look into the various investment options available in the market (Appleby, n.d.).

- 401(k) is the most common retirement option used by people. Apart from retirement planning, it is also used for tax benefits. In this scheme, employees make a contribution through automatic deductions, in some cases the employers match the contribution. If your employer is matching your contribution, then you should aim to contribute to the maximum limit, as this will add to your retirement funds without any additional contribution from your pocket. In 2021, the individual contribution limit was $19,500 to your 401(k), or $26,000 in case you are 50 and above. The combined employer and employee contribution limit is $58,000 and $64,000 if your age is 50 or older.

- Solo 401(k) is for business owners with no employees or self-employed people. In 2021, the contribution limit was $58,000, with a catch up contribution of $6,500 for people aged 50 years and above. The only exception to the no-employee condition is that you can count your spouse as your employee and thus increase your contribution to the IRA. When it comes to the tax deductions model, you have an option to go for a traditional IRA or Roth IRA. Under traditional IRA, the contributions are tax deductible, hence reducing your taxable income. But your withdrawals will be treated as income and hence will be taxed. In the case of Roth IRA, the contributions are part of your income and hence there is no tax break. But your withdrawals later are tax-free. You can open your solo 401(k) account at a bank or a broking firm. For a broking firm, you may require an employee identification number.
- Roth 401(k) is a retirement account that combines the benefits for 401(k) and Roth IRA. It is essentially a savings account that is sponsored by the employer and includes funds that are available post-taxes. This investment tool is ideal for people who think that

their income will be in a higher tax bracket during their retirement than they are now. In this plan they will not have to pay taxes on their withdrawals post-retirement. In short, the contribution and withdrawals are tax-free provided certain conditions are met. The two conditions are that the contributors have an opened Roth IRA account for a minimum of five taxable years. The second condition is that the account owner is permanently disabled, is 59 and a half years old, making withdrawals from an inherited account, or removes $10,000 to buy their first house. If these conditions are met, then the withdrawal is deemed as a qualified distribution and hence is tax-free. You can contribute up to $19,500 and an additional $6,500 if you are 50 years or older (Kagan, n.d.).

- Traditional IRA is an individual retirement account in which the income tax can be deferred. During your retirement, when you make withdrawal from your traditional IRA, you pay income tax. You can open IRA accounts in a brokerage firm or a bank. With a brokerage firm, you can invest in the stock market and bonds. In the case of a bank, you can open a savings account or certificate of deposits. It is advised to invest in stock markets and markets, as historically, they have given higher rates of interest compared to CDs and savings accounts. In 2020 and 2021, the contribution limit was $6,000 and $7,000 if you are aged 50 years and above. The catch here is that you should be a salaried employee in order to be able to contribute to an IRA. You cannot withdraw any money until you have reached the age of 59 and a half, and you may be charged a penalty of 10% in case you have withdrawn earlier than the age limit. It is not compulsory to start withdrawing once you have reached the age limit of 59 and a half; you can wait but you have to start withdrawing required minimum distributions (RMD). You may be able to avoid an early withdrawal penalty if you require money for college, buying a house, medical expenses, and other reasons. The age limit for RMD is 72 or 70 and a half, in case you reached that age in 2019. A penalty as high as 50% will be levied if you do not take your RMDs on time.

- Roth IRA is an investment option that has no tax on contributions and withdrawals. The limit in 2021 is $6,000 or $7,000 if you are aged 50 years or older. The modified adjusted gross incomes in case of a single income tax filing entity should be below $140,000, and in case of a married couple, the limit is $208,000. In order to be eligible to withdraw money without paying taxes, the individual should be 59 and a half years or older, and should have held the account for five years or higher. In this case, you have any minimum required distributions, so you do not have to remove money from your account. There are no taxes on your withdrawals as you have already paid taxes during your investment (O'Shea & Coombes, 2018).

- Simplified Employee Pension is a type of retirement account for self-employed and small business owners. The contributions are tax-deductible and withdrawals are taxed as income. In the case of small business owners, all the employees who have worked for you for three years and have earned $600 in the past one year, then according to the IRS, they are eligible to get a contribution from you. The contribution limit for SEP in 2021 is $58,000. One should also note that the contribution cannot exceed 25% of your compensation or $58,000 in 2021. For people aged 50+, there are no catch-up contributions. Like other IRAs, once you have opened the account, you can invest the amount in CDs, savings account, or stock market and bonds, depending on whether you have opened your account in a bank or with a brokerage firm.

- When deciding your investment options, you may also want to consider the below factors (Probasco, 2020):

1. The age and retirement horizon are some important factors that you should consider while designing your retirement investment portfolio. The retirement horizon over here indicates the time frame you have before you reach your retirement. The earlier you start, with the principle of compound interest, your portfolio will grow stronger. In case you are 50 years and above, you have an option to participate in a plan that has a catch-up contribution feature, and that allows you to increase your contribution to your retirement funds in case you are lagging behind. In 401(k), you can have an option of $6,000 as a catch-up option and in case of IRAs too, you can make a catch-up contribution but it is limited to $1,000. These

additions will allow you to grow your retirement
fund.

2. You should clearly define the purpose of creating a
   retirement account. Usually people open it to fund
   their life post retirement, but in some cases, they also
   open the accounts to leave them behind for their
   families and other beneficiaries. If you are planning
   to leave funds for your beneficiaries, you should
   decide if you want to leave behind tax-free funds or
   if you aim to avoid taking the required minimum
   distributions, as they reduce the account balance.
   Roth IRA and Roth 401(k) offer withdrawals that are
   tax-free. Also, the RMD rules do not apply in case of
   Roth IRA, hence you can leave a larger amount for
   your beneficiaries.

- The final step in your retirement planning is to
  design your retirement portfolio. It is generally
  advised to have an aggressive approach when you are
  younger, and adopt a more conservative approach
  when you are approaching your retirement.
  Investing heavily in stock market bonds during the
  early years will provide you the benefit of compound
  interest and increase your savings. Also, in case you
  suffer some losses in the stock market, you will have
  age in your favour to recover from the losses. Use
  modern services like robo-advisors, start investing in
  the stock market, or you have an option of going
  traditional, take the services of a financial advisor.

HEALTHCARE PLANNING

Healthcare is one of the most significant expenses that an individual may have to incur in their lifetime. It is estimated that an individual who is 65 years old and who retired in 2020 may spend $295,000 in healthcare during the course of their retirement. Even in cases where people have been planning for their retirement throughout their lives, they were not prepared both mentally and financially for healthcare expenses. According to a report, only 51% aged over 60 years believe that their retirement funds will suffice throughout their retirement (Lake, n.d.).

The amount that you will require for healthcare during your retirement depends on your age and overall health. If you have maintained a healthy lifestyle during your younger days and are considerably fit at the time of your retirement, you will spend less on your healthcare during your retirement. On the other hand, maintaining a healthy lifestyle would result in increased life expectancy, hence you will require your retirement funds to last that long.

Relying on Medicare alone to sustain your retirement is not advisable. The important thing to note is that in the case of disabled people or people who depend on others for their well-being, in short the cost of long-term care is not covered by Medicare. If your Medicare does not have a part D, it will not cover your prescription drugs. While relying on Medicare to fund your health expenses during retirement, you will also need to consider the expenses like deductibles, premiums, and other out-of-pocket expenses. Also, dental and vision care expenses are not included in part A and part B.

Another plan called Medicare Advantage, which is offered by private insurers, covers all the expenses that original Medicare covers along with Part D expenses. Some of the Medicare Advantage plans also cover dental and vision care.

Apart from Medicare, there are other ways that individuals can create a corpus fund for their medical expenses.

Health Savings Account, or HSA, is a tax saving healthcare account for people that fund their medical expenses through high-deductible health plans (HDHPs). HDHPs are insurance schemes that have a high minimum deductible for medical expenses. This type of insurance is useful for healthy people who require coverage only in case of serious medical emergency. The advantage with HDHP is that it allows the individual to open an HSA account, where they can make contributions that are tax-deferred. These contributions will help to cover the highly qualified medical expenses that are not covered by HDHP. If the withdrawals from HSA are utilised to cover medical expenses for serious disease, the withdrawals will be exempted from tax deductions. This account is usually opened by people with high income as the deductible is high. The contributions made to HSA can also be used to cover expenses like dental, vision care, and prescription drugs. With the Coronavirus pandemic in picture, a new act, the Coronavirus Aid, Relief, and Economic Security (CARES) Act, was passed in 2020, that allows the HSA funds to be used for over the counter drugs without any prescription. In addition to this, HSA also offers some tax benefits, which includes:

- Deductible contributions
- Tax-deferred growth

- Tax-free withdrawals for qualified medical expenses

The contribution to regular HSA in 2021 is $3,600 for an individual and for families, the contribution can be doubled to $7,200. For people over 55 years, you can make a catch-up contribution of $1,000 per year. An important point to note here is that people who have an Medicare account can longer make new contributions to HSA.

Long-term insurance can be bought to pay a monthly contribution towards the long term for a specified period that can be anywhere between two to five years or for the remaining lifetime. Not everyone can afford this insurance plan, hence it is advised that young people can opt for a long-term insurance rider. The sooner one buys long-term insurance, the cheaper the premiums would be.

Hence, medical expenses are a major part of retirement planning. The more carefully adopted this aspect in their retirement planning, the lesser amount from the retirement fund meant for your other needs will be utilised in your medical emergency.

REVIEW

Leave a 1-Click Review!

I would be incredibly thankful if you could take just 60 seconds to write a brief review on Amazon, even if it's just a few sentences!

CONCLUSION

Personal financial planning is an umbrella concept under which we have smaller concepts like budgeting, investing, savings, insurance buying, debt management, and retirement planning. Writing a clear budget will help to understand your current financial situation, build an emergency fund, and also plan for your retirement. A clear debt management policy will allow you to retire debt-free and also reduce your credit card bills payment. Having the right kind of insurance for various entities like your home and medical insurance will help you to take care of expenses related to these entities. Life insurance will allow your family and beneficiary to continue living the same lifestyle.

Financial planning will force you to have a more disciplined approach towards managing your money. It will help you to identify the mindless spending areas and divert that money to more fruitful actions like upskilling yourself or saving money for your down payment. In short, with proper financial planning you can live happily today and also secure your future.

GIFT

Just For You!

A FREE GIFT TO OUR READERS
Tips for managing your personal finance that you can
download and begin to implement right away! Visit this link:

http://oainc.activehosted.com/f/1

REFERENCES

Appleby, D. (n.d.). The Best Retirement Plans. Investopedia. https://www.investopedia.com/articles/retirement/08/best-plan.asp

Araujo, M. (n.d.-a). Understanding What Home Insurance Policies Cover of Your Belongings. The Balance. https://www.thebalance.com/understanding-what-home-contents-insurance-covers-4135735#are-contents-covered-when-moving

Araujo, M. (n.d.-b). What Is Covered Peril in Homeowner's Insurance? The Balance. https://www.thebalance.-com/homeowners-insurance-peril-2645726#how-does-covered-peril-work

Argyle, M., & Furnham, A. (2013). The Psychology of Money. In Google Books. Routledge. https://books.-google.no/books?id=nVmzA-QAAQBAJ&pg=PA111&lpg=PA111&dq=Why+Do+People+Save?+Attitudes+to (Original work published 2021)

Bank of America. (2018). Saving Money Tips - 8 Simple Ways to Save Money. Better Money Habits. https://better-moneyhabits.bankofamerica.com/en/saving-budget-ing/ways-to-save-money

Beattie, A. (n.d.). Digging Your Way Out of Debt in 8 Steps. Investopedia. https://www.investopedia.com/personal-finance/digging-out-of-debt/

Blokhin, A. (2019). State Income Tax vs. Federal Income Tax: What's the Difference? Investopedia. https://www.investo-pedia.com/ask/answers/060515/what-difference-between-state-income-tax-and-federal-income-tax.asp

Borzykowski, B. (2020, October 22). The ultimate retirement planning guide for 2021. CNBC. https://www.cnbc.-com/guide/retirement-planning/#how-much-do-you-need-to-save-for-retirement

Budgeting | Bank Workers Charity. (n.d.). Www.bwchari-ty.org.uk. https://www.bwcharity.org.uk/guides/mon-ey/budgeting?
gclid=CjwKCAjwqcKFBhAhEiwAfEr7zaz3mkf-SLk9cnvyN-GuO40Bs5k_-ISkkrxVYph-mJ509IfGtBbeUHRoCzCw-QAvD_BwE

Bungalow | Great Homes. Flexible Leasing. Roommate Living. (n.d.). Bungalow.com. https://bungalow.com/arti-cles/how-to-make-a-personal-budget-in-8-easy-steps-plus-tips-for-actually-using

Caldwell, M. (n.d.). A 6-Step Guide to Paying Off Your Debt. The Balance. https://www.thebalance.com/how-to-set-up-a-debt-payment-plan-2385869

Caplinger, D. (n.d.-a). How to Invest in Index Funds: A Beginner's Guide. The Motley Fool. https://www.fool.com/investing/how-to-invest/index-funds/

Caplinger, D. (n.d.-b). What is the S&P 500 Index & How Do I Use It? The Motley Fool. https://www.fool.com/investing/stock-market/indexes/sp-500/

CFP, M. F. (2020, October 5). How to Invest in Stocks. The Motley Fool. https://www.fool.com/investing/how-to-invest/stocks/

Chang, E. (2019). Investing in Stocks for Beginners. US News & World Report; U.S. News & World Report. https://money.usnews.com/investing/investing-101/articles/investing-in-stocks-for-beginners

Cornfield, J. (2020, June 2). 5 things all super savers do that you can actually learn. CNBC. https://www.cnbc.com/2020/06/02/heres-how-you-can-learn-the-simple-habits-of-great-savers.html

Debtor. (2019). Investopedia. https://www.investopedia.com/terms/d/debtor.asp

DeMatteo, M. (2020, July 26). There's "a lot of life to live" before age 59: How to invest your savings for both short- and long-term goals. CNBC. https://www.cnbc.com/select/how-to-invest-savings-short-long-term-goals/

Department, T. (n.d.). 2008 ANNUAL REPORT TO THE PRESIDENT of the PRESIDENT'S ADVISORY COUNCIL ON FINANCIAL LITERACY. https://www.treasury.gov/about/organizational-structure/offices/Domestic-Finance/Documents/PACFL_Draft-AR-0109.pdf

Dore, K. (n.d.). The 6 Best Budgeting Apps of 2021. Investopedia. Retrieved July 22, 2021, from https://www.investopedia.com/best-budgeting-apps-5085405#final-verdict

Elder, H. (1999). Does retirement planning affect the level of retirement satisfaction? Financial Services Review, 8(2), 117–127. https://doi.org/10.1016/s1057-0810(99)00036-0

Fernando, J. (2021, February 2). Bond. Investopedia. https://www.investopedia.com/terms/b/bond.asp

Friedberg, B. (n.d.). How to Invest at Every Age. The Balance. https://www.thebalance.com/how-to-invest-at-every-age-4148023

Gitman, L. J., Joehnk, M. D., Smart, S., & Juchau, R. H. (2015). Fundamentals of Investing. In Google Books. Pearson Higher Education AU. https://books.google.no/books?hl=en&lr=&id=DB3iBAAAQBAJ&oi=fnd&pg=PP1&dq=investing+in+shares&ots=KjX6azopdJ&sig=jtQGWblnO_7Q4zIOBeHz3DlguCk&redir_esc=y#v=onepage&q=investing%20 in%20shares&f=false (Original work published 2021)

Guthrie, C. P., & Nicholls, C. M. (2015). The Personal Budget Project: A practical introduction to financial literacy. Journal of Accounting Education, 33(2), 138–163. https://doi.org/10.1016/j.jaccedu.2015.04.002

Harkness, B. (2018). How to Pay Off Debt: 6 Strategies That Work - Credit Card Insider. Credit Card Insider. https://www.creditcardinsider.com/learn/reducing-debt/

Hayes, A. (2021, April 21). Stock. Investopedia. https://www.investopedia.com/terms/s/stock.asp

How Inflation Affects Your Savings. (2019). Investopedia. https://www.investopedia.com/articles/invest-ing/090715/how-inflation-affects-your-cash-savings.asp

How to Make a Zero-Based Budget. (n.d.). Ramsey Solutions. https://www.ramseysolutions.com/budgeting/how-to-make-a-zero-based-budget

Hyett, N. (n.d.). How to pick shares. Hargreaves Lansdown. Retrieved July 13, 2021, from https://www.hl.-co.uk/shares/how-to-pick-shares

Importance Of Financial Planning. (n.d.). Franklin Templeton Investments. https://www.franklintempletonin-dia.com/investor/investor-education/video/importance-of-financial-plannng-io04og31

Insurance. (2021, July 13). Wikipedia. https://en.wikipedia.org/wiki/Insurance#Legal

Introduction to Investing. (n.d.). Edelweiss. https://www.edelweiss.in/investology/introduction-to-investing-c6eaf4/what-is-investing-basics-for-beginners-c62833

Irby, L. (n.d.). 10 Strategies for Paying Off Your Debt When You're Broke. The Balance. https://www.thebalance.-com/how-to-pay-off-debt-when-you-re-broke-3875583

Irby, L. (2011). How to Manage Debt of Any Size. The Balance. https://www.thebalance.com/how-to-manage-your-debt-960856

Jagannathan, R., & Kocherlakota, N. R. (n.d.). Why Should Older People Invest Less in Stocks Than Younger People? Citeseerx.ist.psu.edu. Retrieved July 17, 2021, from https://citeseerx.ist.psu.edu/viewdoc/download? doi=10.1.1.141.7194&rep=rep1&type=pdf

Kagan, J. (n.d.-a). Roth 401(k). Investopedia. https://www.investopedia.com/terms/r/roth401k.asp

Kagan, J. (n.d.-b). What Is a Debt Snowball? (T. J. Catalano, Ed.).   Investopedia. https://www.investopedia.com/terms/s/snowball.asp

Kagan, J. (2019a). Credit Score. Investopedia. https://www.investopedia.com/terms/c/credit_score.asp

Kagan, J. (2019b). Employee Savings Plan Definition. Investopedia.   https://www.investopedia.com/terms/e/employee-savings-plan.asp

Kagan, J. (2019c). Income Tax Definition. Investopedia. https://www.investopedia.com/terms/i/incometax.asp

Kagan, J. (2019d). Retirement Planning. Investopedia. https://www.investopedia.com/terms/r/retirement-planning.asp

Kagan, J. (2020, November 27). What Is Mortgage Insurance? (E. Rasure, Ed.). Investopedia. https://www.investopedia.com/terms/m/mortgage-insurance.asp

Keim, D. B. (1999). An analysis of mutual fund design: the case of investing in small-cap stocks11I have benefited from generous access to the portfolio managers and trade room personnel at Dimensional Fund Advisors. Thanks also to Marshall Blume, David Booth, Truman Clark, Gene Fama, Gene Fama, Jr., Ken French, Ananth Madhavan, David Musto, Jay Ritter, Rex Sinquefield, and Mitchell Petersen (the referee) for helpful comments and discussions. Journal of

Financial Economics, 51(2), 173–194. https://doi.org/10.1016/s0304-405x(98)00049-x

Kumok, Z. (n.d.). How to Invest at Every Age. Investopedia. https://www.investopedia.com/articles/investing/090915/are-your-investments-right-your-age.asp

Lake, R. (n.d.-a). How to Plan for Medical Expenses in Retirement. Investopedia. https://www.investopedia.com/retirement/how-plan-medical-expenses-retirement/

Lake, R. (n.d.-b). Where to Save Money If You're a Member of Gen Z. The Balance. https://www.thebalance.com/where-to-save-money-if-you-re-a-member-of-gen-z-4589136

Langager, C. (2019). A Beginner's Guide to Stock Investing. Investopedia. https://www.investopedia.com/articles/basics/06/invest1000.asp

Lansdown, H. (n.d.). How to pick shares. Hargreaves Lansdown.

Lea, S. E. G., Webley, P., & Walker, C. M. (1995). Psychological factors in consumer debt: Money management, economic socialization, and credit use. Journal of Economic Psychology, 16(4), 681–701. https://doi.org/10.1016/0167-4870(95)00013-4

Life Insurance Quote. (n.d.). My Finance Helper. https://www.myfinancehelper.com/life-insurance-quote/?gclid=Cj0KCQjw78yFBhCZARIsAOxgSx23lh2AKLwx8I-xax9rU5qg40xQPnT2NwwbO0bzOX2SZk8oa2s88QaAim-TEALw_wcB

Living Within Your Means - Wells Fargo. (n.d.). www.wellsfargo.com. https://www.wellsfargo.com/financial-education/basic-finances/build-the-future/setting-goals/live-within-means/

Livingstone, S. M., & Lunt, P. K. (1992). Predicting personal debt and debt repayment: Psychological, social and economic determinants. Journal of Economic Psychology, 13(1), 111–134. https://doi.org/10.1016/0167-4870(92)90055-c

Marquand, B., & Bundrick, H. M. (2021, March 10). What Is Mortgage Insurance? How It Works, When It's Required. NerdWallet. https://www.nerdwallet.com/article/mortgages/what-is-mortgage-insurance

Mastery, P. L. (n.d.). How To Budget Your Money. www.youtube.com. https://www.youtube.com/watch?v=VfhmzqDHM4w

Mendez, S. (2020, May 26). What does personal possessions cover? - Admiral.com. Www.admiral.com. https://www.admiral.com/magazine/guides/home/personal-possessions-cover-what-youre-covered-for-away-from-home

Mitchell, O. S., & Lusardi, A. (2011). Financial Literacy and Retirement Planning in the United States. SSRN Electronic Journal. https://doi.org/10.2139/ssrn.1810550

Mortgage insurance. (2021, June 4). Wikipedia. https://en.wikipedia.org/wiki/Mortgage_insurance

My Money Coach. (2000). What is Budgeting and Why is it Important? | My Money Coach. Mymoneycoach.ca. https://www.mymoneycoach.ca/budgeting/what-is-a-budget-planning-forecasting

O'Shea, A. (2021, June 30). What Is a Brokerage Account and How Do I Open One? NerdWallet. https://www.nerdwallet.com/article/investing/what-is-how-to-open-brokerage-account

O'Shea, A., & Coombes, A. (2018, April 30). What Is a Roth IRA? How to Get Started - NerdWallet. NerdWallet; Nerd-Wallet. https://www.nerdwallet.com/article/investing/what-is-a-roth-ira

O'Shea, A., & Davis, C. (2021, June 29). How to Start Investing in Stocks: A Beginner's Guide. NerdWallet. https://www.nerdwallet.com/article/investing/how-to-invest-in-stocks#Learn%20the%20difference%20between%20investing%20in%20stocks%20and%20funds.

Orem, T. (2021, May 8). Complete Guide to Retirement Planning: Everything You Need to Know. NerdWallet. https://www.nerdwallet.com/article/investing/retirement-planning-an-introduction

Pant, P. (n.d.-a). 7 Tips for Building an Emergency Fund. The Balance. https://www.thebalance.com/easy-ways-to-build-emergency-fund-453608

Pant, P. (n.d.-b). How to Get Into the Habit of Saving More Money. The Balance. https://www.thebalance.com/getting-into-money-saving-habit-4125552

PhD, G. A. A., & PhD, T. A. B. (2003). Retirement: Reasons, Processes, and Results. In Google Books. Springer Publishing Company. https://books.google.no/books?hl=en&lr=&id=UsAd_P0oH_sC&oi=fnd&pg=PA53&dq=retirement+planning&ots=DX4e9g9tOB&sig=7d7x9N1QNoyIQVnU7Qa1W84nlno&redir_esc=y#v=

onepage&q=retirement%20planning&f=false (Original work published 2021)

Probasco, J. (2020). How Much Do I Need to Retire? (D. Kindness, Ed.). Investopedia. https://www.investopedia.com/retirement/how-much-you-should-have-saved-age/

Rakoczy, C. (n.d.). How to Plan for Discretionary, Variable, and Fixed Expenses In Your Budget. The Balance. https://www.thebalance.com/discretionary-expense-definition-1293678#citation-1

Royal, J. (2019, November). 15 best investments in 2019. Bankrate; Bankrate.com. https://www.bankrate.com/investing/best-investments/

Schulte, T. (2020, July 13). 11 Insanely Easy Ways to Save Money. Define Financial. https://www.definefinancial.com/blog/ways-save-money/

Simple ways to save money - Moneysmart.gov.au. (n.d.). Moneysmart.gov.au. https://moneysmart.gov.au/saving/simple-ways-to-save-money

Smith, L. (2019). How People Fall Into a Debt Spiral. Investopedia. https://www.investopedia.com/articles/pf/12/the-debt-spiral.asp

Spenders vs Savers in Relationships | Signature Wealth. (2018, November 2). Signature Wealth Strategies. https://signaturewealth.com/relationships-spenders-vs-savers/

Staff, T. A. (2019, May 21). Study: The Psychological Cost of Debt | The Ascent. The Motley Fool. https://www.fool.com/the-ascent/research/study-psychological-cost-debt/

The three habits of successful savers. (2014). https://financialhealthexchange.org.uk/wp-content/uploads/2015/11/Which_the-three-habits-of-successful-savers-how-learning-from-their-behaviour-could-get-the-uk-saving_Aug-2014.pdf

Town, P. (2018, December 21). How to Invest Money: A Guide to Grow Your Wealth in 2019 | Rule #1... Rule One Investing. https://www.ruleoneinvesting.com/blog/how-to-invest/how-to-invest-money/

2019 401(k) Participant Survey. (2019). https://content.schwab.com/web/retail/public/about-schwab/schwab-401%28k%29-study-2019_media-deck_0519-975C.pdf

Twin, A. (2019). How Property Insurance Provides Owners Protection. Investopedia. https://www.investopedia.com/terms/p/property-insurance.asp

Urosevic, M. (2020, January 1). 21+ American Savings Statistics to Know in June 2020. SpendMeNot. https://spendmenot.com/blog/american-savings-statistics/

Vansomeren, L. (2011). How to Manage Your Budget Using the 50/30/20 Budgeting Rule. The Balance. https://www.thebalance.com/the-50-30-20-rule-of-thumb-453922

VOHWINKLE, J. (2019). Your 6-Step Guide to Making a Personal Budget. The Balance. https://www.thebalance.com/how-to-make-a-budget-1289587

Vohwinkle, J. (2009, July 23). Basic Budgeting Tips Everyone Should Know. The Balance; The Balance. https://www.thebalance.com/budgeting-101-1289589

Weliver, D. (n.d.-a). How To Get Out of Debt On Your Own: A DIY Guide. Money under 30. https://www.moneyunder30.com/get-out-of-debt-on-your-own

Weliver, D. (n.d.-b). How To Invest Money: The Smart Way To Grow Your Money. Money under 30. https://www.moneyunder30.com/how-to-invest

Weston, L. (2021, March 13). When Can I Retire? NerdWallet. https://www.nerdwallet.com/article/investing/when-can-i-retire

What Affects Your Credit Scores? (2017, May 31). Experian.com. https://www.experian.com/blogs/ask-experian/credit-education/score-basics/what-affects-your-credit-scores/

What Is a Good Credit Score? (2019, April 8). Experian.com. https://www.experian.com/blogs/ask-experian/credit-education/score-basics/what-is-a-good-credit-score/

Woods. (2016, August 25). Not Saving? These 3 Reasons to Save Money Will Give You the Motivation to... Discover Bank - Banking Topics Blog; Discover Bank. https://www.discover.com/online-banking/banking-topics/3-reasons-to-save-more-money/